CLASSIC NEEDLEWORK

CREATE OVER TWENTY PATTERNS FROM THE PAST

CLASSIC NEEDLEWORK

CREATE OVER TWENTY PATTERNS FROM THE PAST

IMOGEN STEWART & SALLY SAUNDERS

STUDIO EDITIONS
LONDON

Classic Needlework
First published in 1992 by Studio Editions Ltd.
Princess House, 50 Eastcastle Street, London W1N 7AP.

Copyright © 1992 Studio Editions Ltd.

The rights of Imogen Stewart and Sally Saunders to be identified as
authors of this work have been asserted by them in accordance with
the Copyright, Designs and Patents Act, 1988.

ISBN 1 85170 943 6

Design and typesetting by Playne Books

Printed and bound in Great Britain

Acknowledgements

The publishers would like to thank the following for their help in the
compilation of this book: Dennis Hawkins and Helen Williams for
colouring the charts; Ann Brown, Anne Hart, Rona Kemp, Jane Lewis,
Susan Morlock, Janet Sears and The Tapestry Centre, Alresford for
their help in working up the finished pieces of embroidery; Raymond
How and Pippa Welbourn, The Oak House Restaurant, Tetbury; Lynn
Szygenda, The Embroiderers' Guild, Hampton Court;
Ken Smith Photography (Edinburgh).

They would also like to thank the following for their kind permission
to reproduce the pictures in this book: The Trustees of the Board of
the Victoria & Albert Museum for the pictures appearing on pages
14, 35, 50, 70, 99, 110 and 114; Traquair House, Peeblesshire for
the pictures appearing on pages 26, 28 and 29; The National Trust
for the pictures appearing on pages 7, 10 and 44 (© The National
Trust 1992); Christie's Colour Library for the pictures appearing on
pages 6, 62 and 90 (© Christie's); The Embroiderers' Guild, Hampton
Court Palace for the pictures appearing on pages 86 and 106; The
Metropolitan Museum of Art, New York for the pictures appearing
on page 80 (gift of Mrs J. Insley Blair); Museum of Fine Arts, Boston
(Seth K. Sweetser Fund) for the picture appearing on page 11; Temple
Newsam House (Leeds City Art Galleries) for the pictures appearing
on page 11 (below); Spink & Son Ltd. for the picture appearing
on page 9.

Photograph opposite title page
*This design has been worked on a
canvas of 16 stitches to 2.5cm (1in).
In this instance the needleworker
has chosen to adapt the chart,
working three of the oranges in wool
number 474, and one in 476. The
chart, however, is the accurate
representation of the original
embroidery.*

Photograph on contents page
*These two patterns have been
worked on a canvas of 14 stitches
to 2.5 cm (1 in) and made into
pincushions. The cord around the
cushions complements the pink and
green shades in the embroidery.*

Contents

Introduction

Decorative needlework on canvas has been used to embellish textiles in every part of the world for hundreds of years. Embroidery on linen canvas, which is the subject of this book, dates back to the Middle Ages, although little survives from before the sixteenth century. Of the few remaining medieval pieces, one of the most interesting is a twelfth-century chasuble from the Benedictine monastery of St Blasien in the Black Forest area of Germany. Worked in long-armed cross-stitch in coloured silks on linen, it depicts scenes from the Biblical stories of the Old and New Testaments and from the lives of the saints.

Since the sixteenth century needlework has been favoured for all kinds of furnishings as well as for clothes and for dress accessories as it is reasonably hard-wearing and quick to work. In particular it has always been a popular pastime in the colder climates of northern Europe and North America. Because the finished work has almost no drape, but hangs stiffly without folds, it is best used flat so that the design and the skill of execution are shown to best advantage.

Needlework is known by several names, including petit point, gros point, canvas work, needlepoint and tapestry embroidery. As the embroiderer works by counting the threads in the base cloth and inserting the needle in the spaces between them, the size of the stitches is dictated by the structure of the cloth. Greater numbers of stitches to the square inch allow more subtle effects to be created as many more nuances of colour can be included within a small area (see, for example, the Bradford table carpet on page 51). Most embroiderers today, however, work on comparatively open canvas.

To ensure that the threads of the base cloth are not split, 'tapestry needles' with large eyes and blunt tips are used.

While early needles were made from a variety of materials, by the sixteenth century they were predominantly of iron and steel. Spain had a thriving needle-making industry during this period, although other countries soon began to manufacture their own.

The detailed projects which follow this Introduction are based on historical embroideries of the sixteenth to the nineteenth centuries. Information is given about the designs and their sources and about the techniques and materials required for their completion, and is intended to provide both inspiration and background reading to the present-day embroiderer.

A pair of George I embroidered cushion covers.

Materials

The word 'canvas' simply means an unbleached cloth, usually of linen (flax), cotton or hemp, although during the eighteenth century wool was also used. It is woven with a plain weave, so that the cloth is made up of regular squares which can easily be counted with the needle. At one time the coarseness varied from an open cloth with eighteen to twenty warp threads to the inch to a much finer, denser cloth with well over fifty threads to the inch. Since the nineteenth century an open-meshed canvas, with perhaps twenty threads to the inch, has generally been used.

Small pieces of canvas can be worked in the hand, but large pieces are stretched on to a frame. In old examples of embroidery it is sometimes possible to find holes along the sides of the canvas where linen was sewn around the edge. Cords were then sewn on to attach the whole piece to the frame.

Threads and Dyes

Generally speaking, the most commonly used embroidery thread for large pieces of canvas was wool, since it was quicker to work and cheaper than silk, which had to be imported into northern Europe from Italy, Spain and the East. The thickness of the thread varied a great deal. Silk was used for smaller items and, in a cream or fawn colour, might be combined with wool to produce special effects, particularly highlights. Other decorative effects were produced by adding touches of metal thread, beads or occasionally such things as small pieces of painted satin for faces. In the later twentieth century cotton thread has been used, but wool is still the most popular.

The advantages of wool over other threads are numerous. It gives a soft warm texture and can be dyed rich and bright colours in many shades. Vegetable dyestuffs can be difficult to use in quantity and wool takes dye better than many other fibres. After the late 1850s, when newly invented chemical or aniline dyes were established, colours became garish for a time. Then designers started to give thought to harmonious colours again and researched old, natural dye recipes. This led to soft, muted tones, to golds and sage greens.

Natural dyes are fragile, especially green for which blue and yellow were used in combination. An old embroidery may appear to be entirely blue because the yellow has faded from those areas once intended to be green. Modern chemical dyes are far more robust and may be used in a highly flexible way to create colour ranges varying from soft and delicate shades to bright and vibrant ones. The designer can work with them in a skilful manner and the possibilities of achieving a range of colour combinations and grading colour are virtually endless.

Stitches

Some sixteenth-century pieces of canvas work are extremely fine and have up to 600 stitches to the square inch. Many of these pieces are executed in a single type of stitch, usually cross or tent stitch, so

'Fancie of the Fowler'. A late sixteenth-century embroidered cushion cover from Hardwick Hall in Derbyshire.

A detail of an elephant from the Oxburgh hangings. These hangings were worked by Mary Queen of Scots and Bess of Hardwick, while Mary was imprisoned. They were later moved to Oxburgh Hall in Norfolk.

that a very even surface is formed. The embroiderer keeps the size of the stitch regular by counting the warp (downward thread in the cloth) and weft (crosswise thread in the cloth) in the canvas, however fine it is.

Cross-stitch, also called gros point, is worked over one or two warp threads depending on the size of the stitch required. Tent stitch, also called petit point, is a sloping satin stitch worked over the point where one warp and one weft thread cross. Gobelin stitch is sometimes used for filling in the ground of the design and was so named because it was thought to achieve an effect like that of woven tapestry from the looms of the famous French Gobelin factory. Other well-known stitches used in canvas work include satin, crosslet, rococo, eyelet, and Florentine stitch (see page 122). Large areas can be covered quickly in simple stitches even when the canvas is quite fine. The more elaborate stitches are usually used for details or small items, which are deliberately designed as demonstrations of skill.

Design and Inspiration

The first large group of embroideries in Europe, and more particularly in the British Isles, date from the later part of the

sixteenth century. Sizable and important items in a well-furnished room, such as long cushions and table carpets, would be intended partly to display the wealth and power of the family and might include their coats of arms. By contrast there were also exquisite small pin cushions and Bible covers, which were just as valued by their owners for the intricate patterns that engaged the mind. All such pieces were a testimony to the skill of the embroiderers, both professional and amateur. In many cases the two worked together, as the professional would supply the design and help the ladies of the house to start work on a large piece. (This practice continued until the late seventeenth century, by which time more patterns were being supplied and there was less need for the professional to work in a wealthy home.)

The large Elizabethan house employed a number of skilled craftsmen, and the 'broderer', who belonged to a company, was hired either to start a project or to work in the house for a specific period. It is known that Mary Queen of Scots employed a professional broderer, although she was also herself a famous needlewoman. Among the pieces almost certainly sewn by her are the Oxburgh hangings, which were worked with Elizabeth Shewsbury, known as Bess of Hardwick, while Bess's husband the Earl of Shewsbury was Mary's gaoler. Together the queen, her noble companion and their attendants made a series of panels depicting emblems, exotic birds, beasts and plants. The designs were taken from woodcut prints, probably found in several different books of beasts. Some resemble the prints by Conrad Gesner, published in *Icones Animalium* in 1560, and it seems likely that they came from that source. The panels were applied to silk hangings and were taken much later to Oxburgh Hall in Norfolk, for which they are now named.

During her fourteen years of captivity Mary worked many other types of embroidery. In a letter to William Cecil of March 1569, Shewsbury described how the queen and her ladies, Lady Lewiston and Mrs Seton, went every day to his wife's chamber to do needlework and how Mary loved to devise works. There are other contemporary references to her love of colour and her considerable talent. She ordered some of her materials from France, where as a young woman she had been married to the Dauphin and where she would have acquired much of her skill.

Horticulture has always been an important source of inspiration for embroidery design. Motifs were taken from herbals, books of plants not necessarily intended for embroiderers but for gardeners, chemists and for medicinal purposes. These books were kept in every wealthy household. Among the most beautiful was *La Clef des Champs* by Jaques Le Moyne de Morgues, published in London at Blackfriars in 1586. Attention was paid to an accurate study of the plants, their roots, their appearance when in flower and in fruit and the insects which might be found near them. All these elements were then transferred to the embroidery design, as can be seen on the slips on pages 15 and 27.

The first pattern books appear to have been printed in Germany in 1524, followed soon afterwards by similar publications in Italy and France. They tend to come from centres of printing rather than centres of needlework, apart from Venice which is famous for both. No technical information was given until the 1540s when a series of Italian pattern books was issued which included designs for cutwork. In general, however, pattern books of motifs intended specifically for embroiderers were not common until the seventeenth century. One of the most popular was *The Needle's Excellency*, published by James Boler in 1631. It has a long introductory poem by John Taylor entitled 'The Praise of the Needle', which gives some technical information about embroidery. Many of the designs found in early pattern books were taken from pre-existing German or Italian patterns. Detailed technical instructions on each pattern are not found in pattern books until much later.

The designers were resourceful and turned to any source they could find for inspiration. Knot patterns of intertwining lines, found in designs intended for gardeners, carvers and plasterers could be used in a variety of ways; illustrations in Bibles, engravings of pastoral and mythological scenes could be translated into an embroidered picture for a table carpet or supply one figure for a smaller piece. Geometric patterns were also much used. Different types of flame work were very popular and such patterns came to be seen as classics. Always the stitches themselves might be combined in a way which enhanced an interesting pattern.

During the seventeenth century embroidered pictures began to be treated as works of fine art, were framed and hung on the wall. They tended to be small and formed part of the set of accessories worked for the fashionable house. Although engravings continued to provide a source for inspiration, the naive quality of some of the pictures worked in the seventeenth and early eighteenth centuries gives them a charm and humour which is unsophisticated and honest.

While the East had always exerted a distinctive influence on western art, as had the West on eastern design, expanding trade at this time meant that a large number of fine embroidered or painted textiles were imported from the Orient. Pattern books were sent out to India from Europe, and many of the Indian designs started to be drawn for the European market. The Dutch, English and French merchants advised the Indian centres of manufacture about what would sell in Europe. This interchange of ideas led to vital and exotic designs in the late seventeenth and eighteenth centuries, when bright colours and finely drawn, embroidered flowers became part of the fashionably furnished room. Panels very like lacquered furniture were embroidered as wall hangings. Some canvas work panels of this type dating from about 1690 were found during the renovation of a house in Hatton Gardens, London, and are now in the Victoria and Albert Museum. Because they had been covered for years the colours are still in very good condition, and it is clear that their large and exotic flowers have been influenced by eastern art. Similar panels worked

by Lady Julia Calverly in 1717, can now be seen at Wallington Hall, Northumberland, where they have been set into the plaster panels decorating one of the first floor rooms. These panels took Julia three and a half years to work; then, in 1727, she finished a second set of panels for a sixfold screen.

As the shape of furniture changed in the late seventeenth century, when fashionable chairs were given elaborately carved frames, embroidered panels began to be used for upholstery. Some of these took the form of purely decorative designs, while others represented entire scenes. The backs, arms and seats of chairs were all upholstered, though not necessarily with the same design on each. Canvas work pictures, whether used for upholstery or for hanging on the wall in a frame, tended to depict illustrations of classical myths, pastoral scenes, fables or moral subjects in contemporary settings,

A panel of linen canvas, embroidered with coloured wools in tent stitch, English, circa 1720. The ground has never been worked although there are trial patches of tent and cross stitches at the top and bottom.

Panels of embroidery worked by Lady Julia Calverly,
from Wallington Hall, Northumberland, 1727.

and Bible stories. In the eighteenth century, as textile designs became lighter and more floral in style, there was a greater emphasis on the serpentine line in the rococo style.

By the early eighteenth century a school of embroidery was developing in New England. Larger houses were being built and they needed furnishing. The community in North America was now well established and women had more time to spare. They would often work decorative pieces such as canvas work pictures. Originally such pictures would be based on engravings imported from Europe; but one needleworker would then copy from another adding slight variations. Scenes of elegantly dressed people angling and engaged in other pastoral pursuits were especially popular. New England in particular became well known for 'Fishing Pictures'.

Later in the eighteenth century there was a fashion for embroidering the tops of card tables with the cards, counters or coins required for a particular game, which were depicted as if they were real. The work was then fitted to the table top, presumably to deceive guests and certainly to be admired. Most of the surviving examples are in very good condition and do not seem to have been much used. Table games of all kinds were very popular in the eighteenth century. As the

century progressed wealthy people started to go to bed later in the evening and therefore needed entertaining once it was too dark to go out. Many families played cards every evening and card tables were always provided at social gatherings. Some games involved gambling for money.

The inventions that transformed textile machinery in the nineteenth century naturally affected the quality of embroidery. Both technical skill and an imaginative approach to design began to disappear. Needlework consisted mainly of pictures copied from coloured patterns and worked in cross-stitch. This was known as berlin wool work and became the most popular embroidery technique for amateurs during the nineteenth century. It was worked with worsted wools on a coarse canvas with a square mesh. By using a coloured pattern on squared paper, the worker only had to count the squares and apply the right colour (see page 107). Often only one stitch was used, either tent or cross-stitch.

Although worsted work remained fashionable until the late 1820s, by the 1830s berlin patterns were being sold in London at Mr Wilk's leading repository and by the 1840s they were so well established that they had started to eclipse other forms of embroidery. Just as Germany was responsible for exporting the patterns, so too did it provide the initial range of dyed wools. The best were Zepher merino from Saxony, which were dyed in clear tones, and both the pastel shades and the pure white wools were famous. England produced wools which were thicker and stronger. In the late 1850s after the aniline dye range had been introduced, more wool was dyed in England. At first the new dyes tended to produce harsh colours which were fragile and faded easily. Chemical dyes soon improved but the fashion for bright, harsh colours remained until late in the nineteenth century, especially in berlin wool work.

During the 1840s other materials started to be used in conjunction with berlin wools. Silk might be added for highlights; chenille thread could be used to obtain a velvety appearance; and beads of many different kinds were introduced. Designs for berlin wool work worked entirely in beads appear in the 1850s, although bead work itself is a much older technique. At this period designs became larger and a more naturalistic representation of plants and animals came into fashion.

Berlin wool work was also used for pictures, and in many cases for reproductions of the old masters. Leonardo da Vinci's *Last Supper* for example, worked by Mrs Morris, was exhibited at the Great Exhibition held in the Crystal Palace, Hyde Park, in 1851. Embroidered floor carpets or mats had been known since the sixteenth century and continued to be produced throughout the seventeenth and eighteenth centuries. These too were worked in berlin wools during the nineteenth and twentieth centuries. Foot stools, low-seated chairs, prie-dieu and other pieces of occasional furniture were all upholstered in berlin wool work, sometimes by amateurs whose skills might

'The Fishing Lady Chimney Piece'. A needlework picture embroidered by the wife of Colonel Sylvanus Bourne. New England (1740-1770). Wool, silk and metallic yarns, and spangles embroidered on linen canvas. (52.7 x 110.5 cm   20¾ x 43½ in)

The Long Gallery at Temple Newsam House, West Yorkshire, houses a set of mid-eighteenth-century furniture upholstered with embroidery, comprising twenty chairs, four sofas and one day bed.

A detail of the day bed from the Long Gallery at Temple Newsam House in West Yorkshire.

Berlin wool work patterns.

more sensibly have been suited to cushions and other household accessories.

By the second half of the nineteenth century women's journals such as *The Englishwoman's Domestic Magazine* gave many patterns for berlin wool work. These included such items as a sofa cushion, the materials for which cost 5s 6d, brackets for covering unwanted gas lights in the summer and bell pulls, all appropriate furnishings for the kind of cluttered, cosy Victorian interior where servants were needed to dust and clean.

When the fashion was at its height some textile manufacturers even used motifs from berlin patterns for the designs on their printed cotton cloth. Only a few dress accessories were ever produced in canvas work. These consisted mainly of small bags or shoes for ladies. During the great fashion for berlin wool work, however, many

pairs of gentlemen's slippers and braces were worked. Even gentlemen's waistcoats became fashionable at the turn of the nineteenth and twentieth centuries.

The popularity of berlin wool work began to wane in the 1870s, when the Royal School of Art Needlework, the Leek Embroidery Society, Morris & Co. and several ecclesiastical embroidery societies started to draw attention to old techniques and the possibilities offered by other forms of embroidery. These organizations encouraged both amateur and professional designers to take a more individual approach to their work. Then, as the Arts and Crafts Movement sought to revive crafts in the late nineteenth and early twentieth centuries, there was a further revitalization in design. Several eminent teachers of needlework, among them Mrs Grace Christie, broadened the scope of embroidery by emphasizing originality in design and technical skill.

Samplers

Samplers provided a way of learning and recording both different types of stitches and the ways in which they could be combined. Small motifs were also worked on samplers, sometimes partly in one thread and partly in another to demonstrate a variety of effects. Early samplers were probably worked on fragments of linen, but during the second half of the sixteenth century they appear to have developed a far more standard form. This took the shape of a strip of linen canvas, with the selvage at the top and bottom so that the length was the loom width of 48 to 53cm (19 to 21 in) and the width was cut to about 30cm (12 in).

The first known named and dated sampler was probably made by Jane Bostock in 1598 and is now in the Victoria & Albert Museum. At the top Jane has worked a random collection of figurative motifs: plants, a bear, a dog, a deer and a very small lion. A neat row of letters, her name and 1598 follow, some of the letters being worked in seed pearls. Next there is an inscription reading 'Alice Lee was borne the 23 of November being Tuesday in the afternoon 1596'. Perhaps Jane wanted to record the birth of a favourite niece. Not many samplers have this personal interest. They are usually a catalogue of stitches and motifs of the kind Jane used to fill the main part of her sampler. This includes a long list of stitches, not all of which would have been used for needlework.

Gradually the sampler became a neatly worked exercise. Those that were kept demonstrated that the child had reached a certain level of skill. In some girls' schools the best ones were mounted in a book. During the eighteenth and early nineteenth centuries a picture of a house and a text from the Bible or a prayer, were often included and a wide range of stitches were still used, as can be seen in the sampler on page 110. However, by the second half of the nineteenth century, most children worked their samplers only in cross-stitch and did not necessarily learn any of the more complicated stitches. They therefore graduated quite easily to berlin wool work in a single stitch.

A sampler is still a useful way to practise and experiment. Once a certain amount of skill has been acquired the different combinations of motifs and stitches can give endless pleasure.

How to use this book

The pieces of embroidery illustrated in the following pages have been selected both for their historical interest and their beauty. Each original piece is accompanied by a short introduction, practical instructions and a colour chart and key explaining how to recreate the design.

These embroidery projects are arranged in chronological order and cover a wide range of subjects from floral slips and pictorial scenes to repeating patterns. They are of varying complexity, so the Posies (page 107) and the Fruit Trees from Traquair House (page 27), for example, would be suitable projects for the beginner, while the Shepherdess (page 70) and the detail from the Bradford table carpet (page 51) are included for the more ambitious needleworker.

Although embroidery techniques have not changed over the years, embroidery materials have. In the past embroiderers worked on fine canvases with maybe 50 holes to 2.5 cm (1 in) which allowed them to include many shades of wool in each element of the design. The instructions which accompany the pieces of needlework in this book have been adapted to suit the modern-day needleworker; thus, the number of wool colours in each pattern has been reduced and a more open-meshed canvas has been chosen. Moreover, over the years the colours of the threads will have faded. It would also be difficult to match the original historic colours with those currently available on the market. Wool colours for each project have therefore been carefully chosen taking this into account, so that they remain as true as possible to the original, whilst combining well together.

The practical instructions that accompany each project are a step-by-step guide to working up the pattern, with canvas sizes, wool colours, quantities, and stitching instructions. Many of the designs can be adapted to suit your own requirements, especially the repeating patterns or the background colour of the slips. The colours can be changed to suit the colour scheme of your home, or the canvas size can be altered to make a larger or smaller design. For example, in the worked up sample of the Carnation Florentine Pattern the peacock blue wool has been replaced by a brighter green (see page 101). If you do alter the designs, work up a small area first to check that the new colours work well together.

Where the colour charts spread over more than two pages there are arrows to indicate where the next section of the chart appears and a miniature reduction of the complete chart showing the page divisions and the sections fitting together. The centre is marked on each chart with a black cross.

At the end of the book there is a section giving additional information on materials and techniques, on framing and stretching the canvas, stitches, making up cushions and how to adapt the charts.

Cornflowers and Pansies

Two slips depicting cornflowers and pansies. These were worked in England in about 1600 in silk thread on linen canvas, in tent stitch.

Sets of slips were intended for application to furnishings. They were often stitched by amateurs, as they could be worked in the hand or on a small hand frame. Unlike table carpets and other large projects, which had to be worked in a large frame by a group of needlewomen, slips could be carried around and embroidered in odd moments. Slips continued in use until well into the seventeenth century, when they were smaller in scale and were sometimes used in raised work.

The outlines of the motifs were drawn in ink, either individually onto separate small panels of linen or in rows on one larger panel, and were often sewn in black silk cross-stitch. In this case the drawing is simple and the whole outline has been worked, while in other designs the black may be omitted where an area of highlight is required. When coloured silks had been worked and the final stage started, the motif was cut around the edge. Since the linen was often loosely woven and would fray easily, the piece might be stiffened on the back with flour and water paste or with a piece of fine silk or linen. The motifs were then applied to a ground fabric, usually an expensive imported cloth such as silk or velvet. The edges of the motif were tucked underneath and sometimes a silk or metal thread cord was couched on around to hide the join. Thus, if a black outline had been used it would hardly show when the motif had been applied.

INSTRUCTIONS

These delightful designs of cornflowers and pansies lend themselves to being small pictures or cushion inserts. They could be worked on any size of canvas, but a fine canvas will give the dainty appearance of the original pieces of embroidery.

Materials

Single canvas, 16 stitches to 2.5 cm (1 in). You will need 29 x 39 cm (11½ x 15½ in) of canvas which allows for 2.5 cm (1 in) of background around the floral design. Add an extra 7.5 cm (3 in) all around for making up.

Single canvas, 18 or 22 stitches to 2.5 cm (1 in) can be used to give a really fine look similar to the original pieces of work.

Use two or three strands of Appleton crewel wool in the needle depending on your tension. Practise a small area first to see which is sufficient to cover the canvas. If you use three strands allow extra yarn.

The quantities of wool given below are approximate and will vary from person to person. It is important to buy the background wool in hanks, rather than skeins, and that each hank is from the same dye lot. The dye varies slightly from lot to lot and any change will show up on the background. If you do need to buy a second quantity then you should mix the old batch with the new.

Cornflowers

One skein of 123, 187, 251, 322, 324, 328, 354, 564, 565, 691, 876 and 983; two skeins of 992; three skeins of 356, 841 and

These two patterns have been worked on canvas of 18 stitches to 2.5 cm (1 in). Appleton crewel wool number 351 has been used for the background of the cornflowers, and number 961 for the background of the pansies. The piping is made from the backing material of the cushions.

842; six skeins of 159 and three hanks of 351 for the background.

Pansies

One skein of 294, 333, 334, 336, 352, 356, 471, 551, 562, 564, 565, 603, 604, 713, 715, 841, 884 and 992; three skeins of 331; four skeins of 354; six skeins of 358 and three hanks of 961 for the background.

If you wish to use more wool the general rule is that one hank will cover an area of 15 x 15 cm (6 x 6 in).

Size 20 or 22 tapestry needles for 16- and 18-thread canvas; size 22 or 24 for 22-thread canvas. Use a needle which will take the correct number of threads without damaging them, and which will not distort the canvas when stitching.

Method of working

Fold the canvas in half twice to find the centre. Mark the folds with a hard pencil or tacking stitches. For best results, use a square peg or slate frame (see page 121).

Match your threads to the colour chart key and number if necessary. Find the centre of the chart. Each coloured square on the chart represents one tent stitch, worked over a single thread of the canvas (see page 122 for stitching instructions).

Thread a needle with the outline colour, and begin working the outline nearest to the centre of the chart. Knot the end of the thread and take the needle down through the canvas about 5 cm (2 in) from the start of the work. This thread can then be worked over at the back of the canvas as the embroidery progresses, and the knot can be cut off. Finish off threads in the same way by bringing each thread up 5 cm (2 in) from the work and these will be worked in.

Use a length of wool in the needle not longer than 80 cm (32 in). If the thread is too long, it becomes worn and thin as you work and will not cover the canvas properly.

When you have completed the outline around each flower, leaf or stem, fill in the colours as shown on the chart.

Work the background in diagonal tent stitch (see page 122). This gives a better tension than ordinary tent stitch and will not distort the canvas.

Further suggestions

1 If the design is to be made into a picture, use stranded cotton and work the design on a fine canvas, 18 or 22 stitches to 2.5 cm (1 in).

2 Stitch small seed pearls or tiny beads in the centre of each flower and the tips of the petals.

3 For the background, any of the following stitches would give a more textural finish, without being too overpowering: cashmere stitch, Hungarian stitch, chequer stitch, upright cross stitch, straight Gobelin stitch (see page 122). These stitches could be worked in wool or stranded cotton. (Stranded cotton will not wear as well as wool and is more expensive.)

PAGE 18   PAGE 19

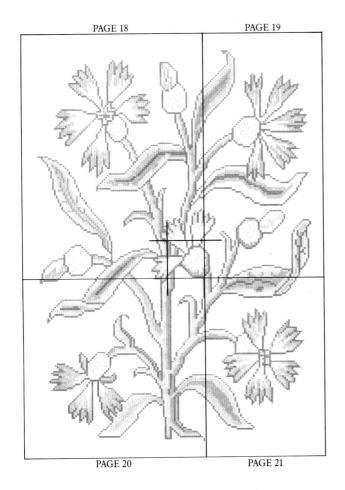

PAGE 20   PAGE 21

PAGE 22   PAGE 23

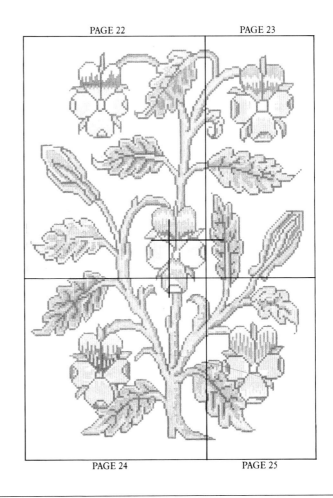

PAGE 24   PAGE 25

PAGE 20 ▽

PAGE 21 ▽

LEAVES AND STEMS	BLUE LEAF	CALYCES	FLOWERS
841	992	324	992
842	876	876	876
251	565	992	322
354	328	123	564
356		187	983
159		691	

Please note: many subtle shades are used in the chart, therefore the colours for each separate element of the design have been listed individually in the key.

PAGE 18 △

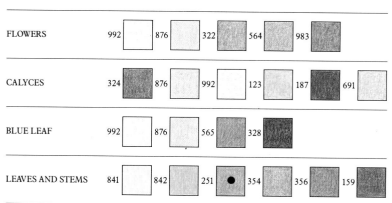

FLOWERS	992		876		322		564		983	
CALYCES	324		876		992		123		187		691
BLUE LEAF	992		876		565		328			
LEAVES AND STEMS	841		842		251	●	354		356		159

PAGE 19 △

Outline stitches in silk were embroidered on the calyces of the original design. These stitches are represented by brown lines on the chart. They should be worked in cotton or silk.

Please note: many subtle shades are used in the chart, therefore the colours for each separate element of the design have been listed individually in the key.

PAGE 24 ▽

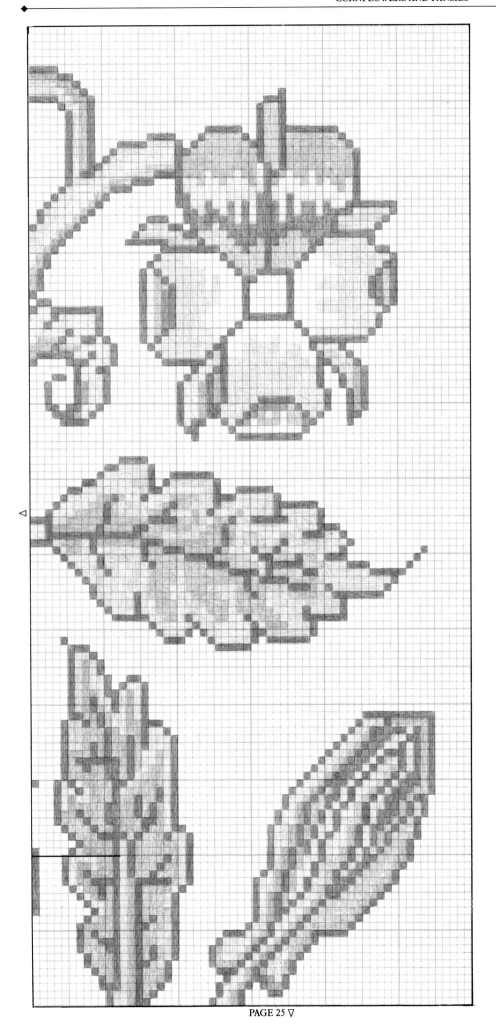

PAGE 25 ▽

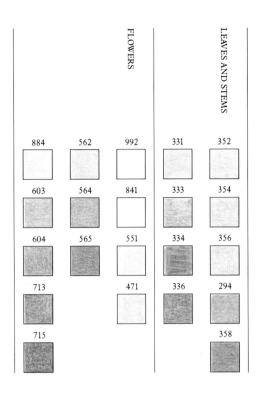

FLOWERS

LEAVES AND STEMS

884	562	992	331	352
603	564	841	333	354
604	565	551	334	356
713		471	336	294
715				358

Please note: many subtle shades are used in the chart, therefore the colours for each separate element of the design have been listed individually in the key.

PAGE 22 △

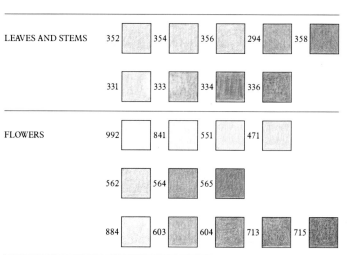

LEAVES AND STEMS	352		354		356		294		358	
	331		333		334		336			

FLOWERS	992		841		551		471			
	562		564		565					
	884		603		604		713		715	

PAGE 23 △

Please note: many subtle shades are used
in the chart, therefore the colours for each
separate element of the design have been
listed individually in the key.

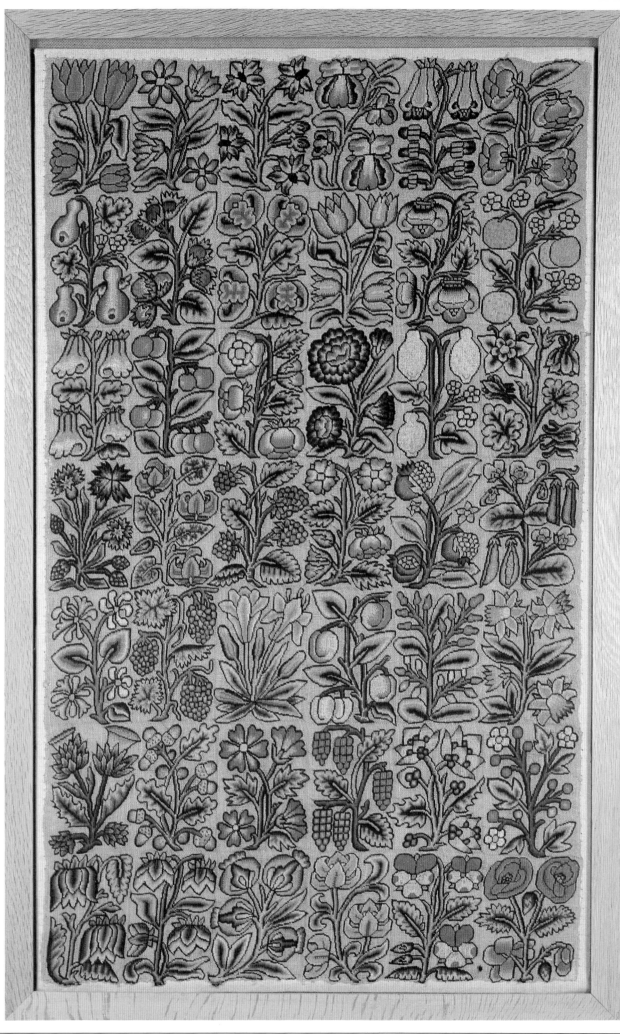

Fruit Trees from Traquair House

A panel of worked slips from Traquair House, Scotland: these are among the most famous sets of slips; they are in fine condition and depict a series of plants popular in the Elizabethan period.

Not all these plants were indigenous to the British Isles. Some demonstrate the Elizabethans' great interest in those newly discovered plants brought back by sixteenth-century explorers. The group of native plants includes some of the most popular both in Elizabethan embroidery and in the garden. They include borage, daffodil, the tulip (which had been imported into Europe in the early sixteenth century and was now well established), thistle, honeysuckle, pansy, sweet peas shown in both pod and flower, poppy, cornflower and the rose. Among the fruits there are oranges shown in fruit and flower, lemons, pears, grapes, the exotic peach and the highly prized strawberry, again depicted in both fruit and flower. At this period the strawberry had a small berry which was considered a very pure fruit. Some gardeners thought that the plant would purify the soil around it. It grew wild but was also planted in orchards, where it powdered the grass with its white flowers. Some inedible plants are also depicted here, such as acorns.

The slips are worked in silk thread on linen canvas and represent hours of work, although their condition suggests that they were never used. The rectangular shape of each one indicates that the designs were taken from woodblock prints. They have been worked very closely together and would have been difficult to cut out. A number of sets of such slips have been found, and it seems likely that in some cases more were made than were needed.

INSTRUCTIONS

These three pieces of embroidery taken from a collection of herbal designs are really delightful and would look good as a set of framed pictures or as cushions.

Materials

Single canvas, 16 stitches to 2.5 cm (1 in). Listed below are the amounts of canvas required to work up the three designs allowing for 2.5 cm (1 in) of background around each one. Their sizes vary slightly; if you would like to make a matched set the amount of background can be altered to even them up. Allow an extra 7.5 cm (3 in) all around for making up.

Grapes	15 x 20 cm	(6 x 8 in)
Oranges	17.5 x 20 cm	(7 x 8 in)
Pears	14 x 20 cm	(5½ x 8 in)

Use two or three strands of Appleton crewel wool in the needle depending on your tension. Practise a small area first to see which is sufficient to cover the canvas. If you use three strands allow extra yarn.

The quantities of wool given below are approximate and will vary from person to person. It is important to buy the background wool in hanks, rather than skeins, and that each hank is from the same dye lot. The dye varies slightly from lot to lot and any change will show up on the background. If you do need to buy a second quantity then you should mix the old batch with the new.

Grapes

One skein of 142, 152, 155, 157, 158, 221, 222, 223, 251, 354, 358, 403, 407, 472, 712, 714, 751, 876, 882, 924, 952 and 955; two skeins of 588 and one hank of 181 for the background.

Oranges

One skein of 185, 222, 251, 305, 403, 405, 407, 472, 474, 475, 476, 542, 702, 753, and 954; two skeins of 588 and one hank of 761 for the background.

Pears

One skein of 152, 155, 158, 187, 315, 405, 407, 471, 472, 475, 542, 543, 697, 702, 767, 861 and 954; two skeins of 473 and 588 and one hank of 691 for the background.

If you wish to extend the background area and use more wool the general rule is that one hank will cover an area of 15 x 15 cm (6 x 6 in).

Size 20 / 22 tapestry needles.

Method of working

Fold the canvas in half twice to find the centre. Mark the folds with a hard pencil or tacking stitches. Ideally use a square peg frame to work the embroidery or alternatively a deep-sided ring frame with a 25 cm (10 in) ring (see page 121).

Match your threads to the colour chart key. Find the centre of the chart. Each coloured square on the chart represents one tent stitch, worked over a single thread of the canvas (see page 122 for stitch instructions).

Thread a needle with the outline colour and begin working the outline nearest to the centre of the chart. Knot the end of the thread and take the needle down through the canvas about 5 cm (2 in) from the start of the work. This thread can then be worked over at the back of the canvas as the embroidery progresses, and the knot can be cut off. Finish off threads in the same way by bringing each thread up 5 cm (2 in) from the embroidery and these will be worked in.

Use a length of wool in the needle not longer than 80 cm (32 in). If the thread is too long, it becomes worn and thin as you work and then will not cover the canvas properly.

When you have completed the outline around each flower, leaf or stem, fill in the colours as shown on the chart.

Work the background in diagonal tent stitch (see page 122). This gives a better tension than ordinary tent stitch and will not distort the canvas.

Further suggestions

1   Use a different stitch for the background. Any of the following stitches would give a more textural finish without being too overpowering: Hungarian stitch, chequer stitch, cashmere stitch, upright cross stitch or straight Gobelin stitch (see page 122).

2   Set each fruit in the centre of a cushion with a border of Florentine stitch (see page 122) all round. Pick out the colours used in the fruit.

Details of the grapes, oranges and pears from the panel of slips at Traquair House in Scotland.

LEAVES	221	472	251	403	407		
MAUVE GRAPES	751	222	223	142	712	714	924
GREEN GRAPES	472	251	354	358			
BLUE LEAF	472	876	152	155	157	158	
STEM	882	952	955	588			

The pears in this picture have been worked on a canvas of 16 stitches to 2.5 cm (1 in).

LEAVES	222	474	472	251	542	403	405	407
BLOSSOM	702	753	222					
ORANGES	474	475	476					
STEM	954	185	305	588				

Please note: many subtle shades are used in the chart, therefore the colours for each separate element of the design have been listed individually in the key.

This design has been worked on a canvas of 17 stitches to 2.5 cm (1 in). The cord around the cushion is made from the pink and purple shades of wool used in the embroidery and the background is worked in Appleton crewel wool number 181.

BLUE LEAF	152	155	158	471	472		
BLOSSOM	702	861					
STEMS	954	767	187	588			
LEAVES	471	472	473	542	543	405	407
PEARS	471	473	475	697	315		

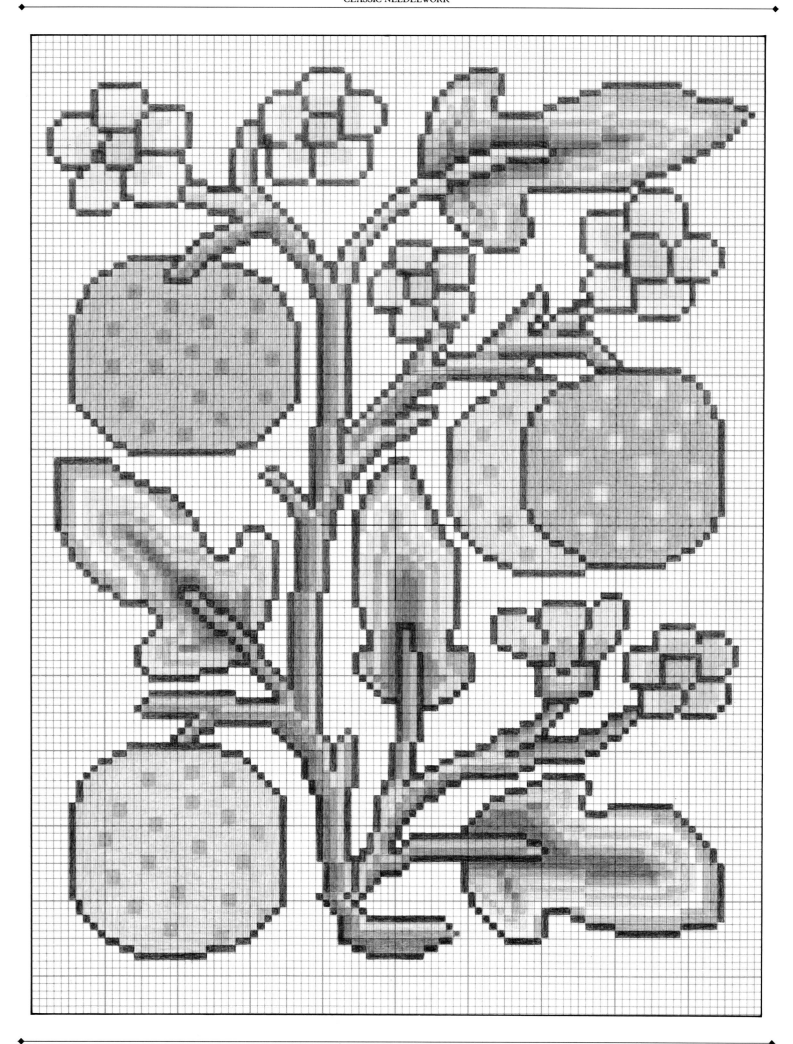

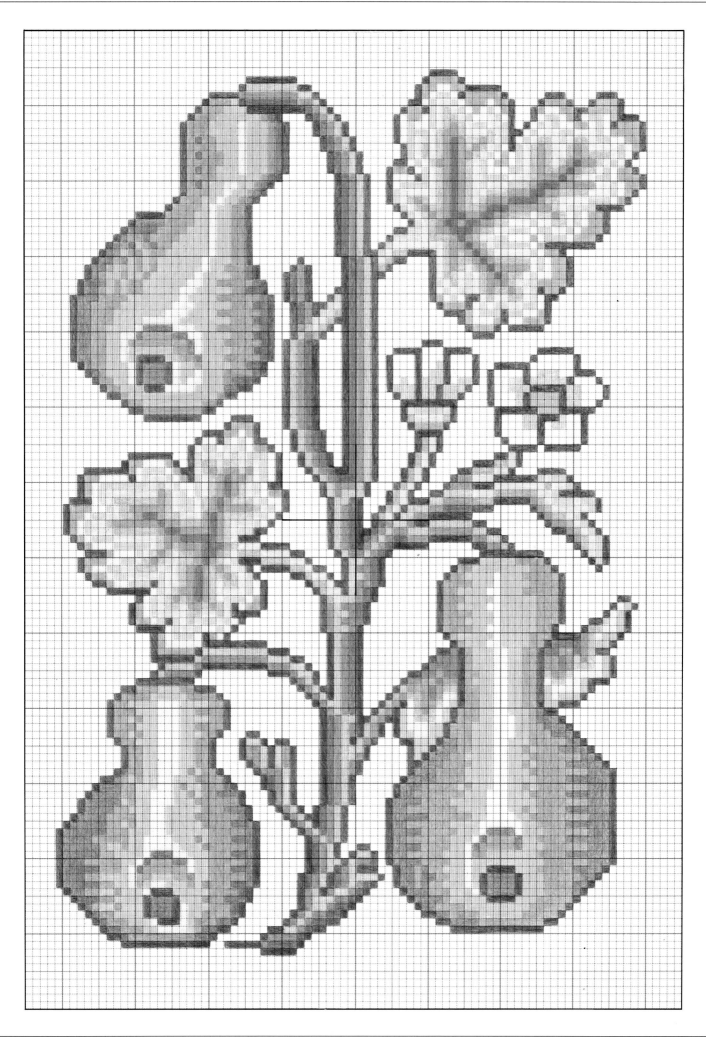

Exotic Birds and Beasts

A panel of motifs for applied work, worked in silk, in tent stitch, on linen canvas. This piece was made in England around 1600, with some small additions worked in wool and silk at some time in the early eighteenth century. These motifs were never used, although others from the same piece have evidently been cut off to be applied elsewhere. While individual patterns have been repeated, each one is worked in different colours, so they may have been intended as a set for applying on cushions or hangings, or used up gradually on different items of furnishings.

The drawing of the motifs is bold and the designs for these birds, fish and insects were probably originally taken from woodblock prints found in a book of beasts. Although it is possible to identify some of the creatures, others, such as the fish, are fantastic. The birds are shown in various positions. One is preening itself, another, a falcon, has caught a small bird.

Wealthy people spent a lot of time hunting. Both Elizabeth I and James I were known to have taken great pleasure in the sport. A small yet comparatively grand house, known as a 'hunting box', was sometimes erected for noble people to hunt from. Hunting scenes and other motifs connected with the sport, such as the falcon, were often recorded in needlework and woven tapestry design.

The colours have been carefully selected to give the creatures an exotic appearance. Graded shades are used to round the forms so that they seem more natural. Glowing colours such as these are typical of applied motifs which have never been used but have been stored away from the light and dirt. When applied to a deeply coloured silk or velvet ground fabric, they must have created an impression of great richness.

INSTRUCTIONS

The three designs shown in this project would look very good worked up as pictures or cushions.

Materials

Single canvas, 14 stitches to 2.5 cm (1 in). Listed below are the amounts of canvas required to work up the three designs allowing for 2.5 cm (1 in) of background around each one. Allow an extra 7.5 cm (3 in) all around for making up.

Fish	22.5 x 19 cm	(9 x 7½ in)
Bird	30.5 x 33 cm	(12 x 13 in)
Parrot	28 x 35.5 cm	(11 x 14 in)

For a really fine embroidery that will give the effect of the original, you should use a smaller-mesh canvas, 16 or 18 stitches to 2.5 cm (1 in).

Use two or three strands of Appleton crewel wool in the needle depending on your tension. Practise a small area first to see which is sufficient to cover the canvas. If you use three strands allow extra yarn.

The quantities of wool given below are approximate and will vary from person to person. It is important to buy the background wool in hanks, rather than skeins, and that each hank is from the same dye lot. The dye varies slightly from lot to lot and any change will show up on the background. If you do need to buy a second quantity then you will need to mix the old batch with the new.

Fish

One skein of 181, 182, 561, 564, 565, 567, 645, 754, 756, 841, 948, 992 and 998 and one hank of 181 for the background.

Bird

One skein of 121, 158, 181, 182, 251A, 252, 333, 473, 542, 561, 564, 565, 567, 752, 754, 841, 948, 956, 973, 992 and 993 and two hanks of 182 for the background.

Parrot

One skein of 183, 184, 223, 542, 752, 754, 757, 842, 957 and 998; two skeins of 473, 561, 564, 643, 645, 647 and 927; three skeins of 992 and two and a half hanks of 181 for the background.

If you wish to use more wool the general rule is that one hank will cover an area of 15 x 15 cm (6 x 6 in).

Size 20 or 22 tapestry needles for 14-, 16- and 18-thread canvas; a size 22 or 24 for 22-thread canvas. Use a needle which will take the correct number of threads without damaging them, and which will not distort the canvas when stitching.

Method of working

Fold the canvas twice to find the centre. Mark the folds with a hard pencil or tacking stitches. Ideally use a square peg frame to work the embroidery or alternatively a deep-sided ring frame with a 25 cm (10 in) ring (see page 121)

Match your threads to the colour chart key. Find the centre of the chart. Each coloured square on the chart represents one tent stitch, worked over a single thread of the canvas (see page 122 for stitching instructions).

Thread a needle with the outline colour and begin working the outline nearest to the centre of the chart. Knot the end of the

thread and take the needle down through the canvas about 5 cm (2 in) from the start of the work. This thread can then be worked over at the back of the canvas as the embroidery progresses, and the knot cut off. Finish off threads in the same way by bringing each thread up 5 cm (2 in) from the embroidery and these can then be worked in.

Use a length of wool in the needle not longer than 80 cm (32 in). If the thread is too long, it becomes worn and thin as you work and will not cover the canvas properly.

When you have completed the outline around one area, fill in the rest of the shape. Work the background in diagonal tent stitch (see page 122). This gives a better tension than ordinary tent stitch and will not distort the canvas.

Further suggestions

1 Use a different stitch for the background. Any of the following would give a more textural finish without being too overpowering — Hungarian stitch, chequer stitch, cross stitch or cashmere stitch (see page 122 for the stitching instructions).

2 Add other stitches to the design. The cherries would look nice worked in upright cross stitch; the stem of the tree in Renaissance stitch worked vertically; the leaves in cross stitch.

3 If creating a picture, add silk highlights to the design on the tips of the feathers, eyes and beak. Silk used on the cherries would have also be effective. Experiment with different threads. Note that silks do not wear as well as wools.

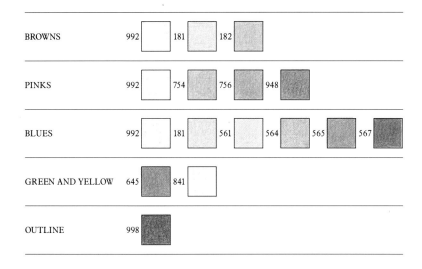

BROWNS	992		181		182				
PINKS	992		754		756		948		
BLUES	992		181		561		564		565		567
GREEN AND YELLOW	645		841	
OUTLINE	998	

MOUND	158		252		542		473		992		
BIRD	948		754		752						
	993		567		565		564		561		992
	956		973		182		121		181		251 A

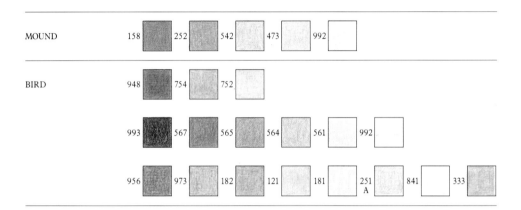

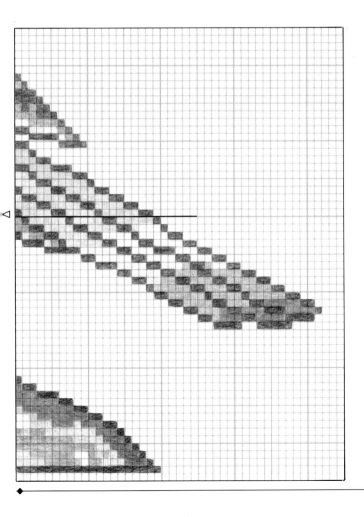

BLUES	992		561		564		927
FAWNS	992		183		184	957	998
GREENS	842	473		542		643	645	647
PINKS	752	754		223		757		

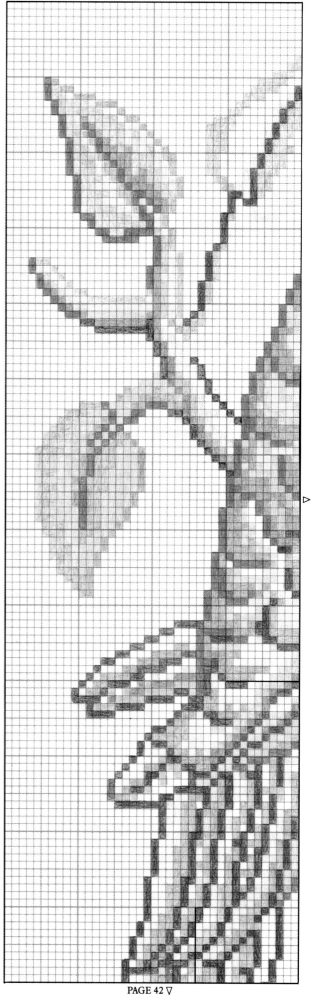

PAGE 42 ▽

PAGE 40   PAGE 41

PAGE 42   PAGE 43

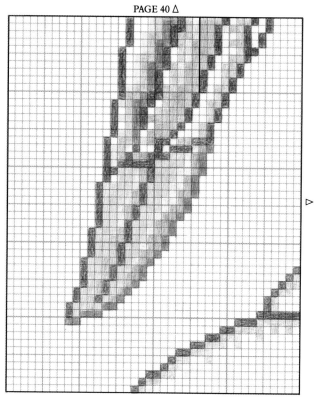

PAGE 40 △

BLUES	992		561		564		927	

FAWNS	992		183		184		957		998	

GREENS	842		473		542		643		645		647	

PINKS	752		754		223		757	

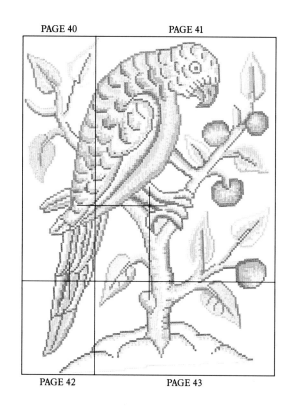

PAGE 40   PAGE 41

PAGE 42   PAGE 43

△

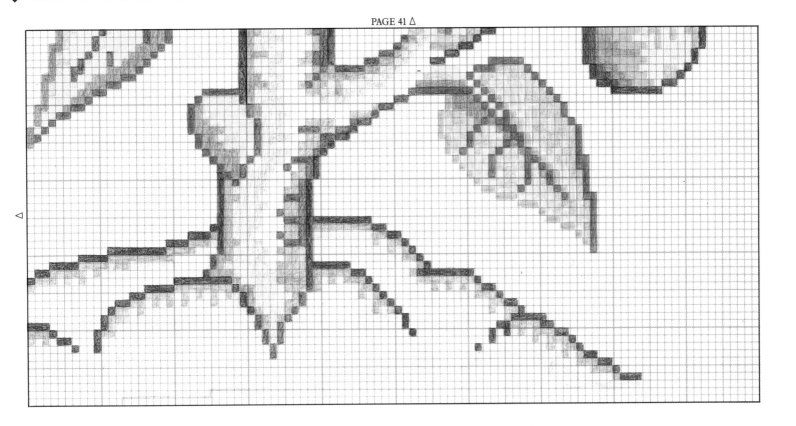

The parrot has been worked on a canvas of 15 stitches to 2.5 cm (1 in). In this instance the needleworker has chosen to drop wool number 643, and to stitch both the lighter greens in number 542 to create a brighter design. The chart, however, reflects the deeper colours of the original seventeenth-century embroidery.

Oak Leaves from Hardwick Hall

A panel of late sixteenth-century needlework from a cushion at Hardwick Hall . (The edge of this cushion is trimmed with a braid which may have been applied later.)

The oak was a very popular motif since it symbolized strength. In this case the leaf has been used in a decorative manner. The motifs are arranged in straight rows, pointing in different directions. This form of design is found in the woven silks imported from Italy during this period and would have been known in great houses. Interest is added to the rows of motifs by slight variations in the details used on each leaf which attract the eye even while the overall design remains very ordered. Geometric patterns or highly stylized floral motifs were also used in this manner. The differences within the leaves have been achieved by skilful use of colour. Although the overall design is restricted to a limited palette, the golds, blacks and greys have been combined to form contrasts and optical illusions. Further contrast is added by the use of long-armed cross-stitch and tent stitch, which create the effect of different textures.

The deep colour and the use of wool embroidery thread must have added warmth in every way to the interior of the house in winter.

INSTRUCTIONS

This charming repeat design of oak leaves looks almost modern. It would look really stunning on a set of dining chairs, or an individual stool top (see page 123 for instructions on making a template). Alternatively the whole design would make a wonderful rug, worked on a coarse canvas, 10 stitches to 2.5 cm (1 in).

Each oak leaf in the original design varies slightly in its colour scheme. A selection of the motifs are shown on the chart on page 48. If you are working up a large project the chart could be repeated or you could continue adding slight variations in the colours.

Materials

Single canvas, 16 stitches to 2.5 cm (1 in). The size of canvas will vary according to how you choose to use the design (see page 123 for instructions on adapting a chart), but you will need 25 x 22.5 cm (10 x 9 in) of canvas to work the area shown on the chart. Allow an extra 7.5 cm (3 in) of canvas all around for making up.

Use two or three strands of Appleton crewel wool in the needle, depending on your tension. Practise a small area first to see which is sufficient to cover the canvas. If you use three strands allow extra yarn.

The quantities of wool needed to work this design will vary according to the number of times you repeat the pattern. The amounts listed below are for the area shown on the chart. It is important to buy the background wool in hanks, rather than skeins, and that each hank is from the same dye lot. The dye varies slightly from lot to lot and any change will show up on the background. If you do need to buy a second quantity then you should mix the old batch with the new.

One skein of 155, 187, 473 and 841; two skeins of 152 and 302; three skeins of 471 and one hank of 866 for the background. Alternatively you can mix 866 and 208, or 865 and 866 for the background, then you will need four skeins of each.

If you wish to use more wool the general rule is that one hank will cover an area of 15 x 15 cm (6 x 6 in).

Size 20/22 tapestry needles.

Method of working

Fold the canvas in half twice to find the centre. Mark the folds with a hard pencil or tacking stitches. Ideally use a square peg frame to work the embroidery, or alternatively a deep-sided ring frame (see page 121).

Match your threads to the colour chart key. Find the centre of the chart. Each coloured square on the chart represents one tent stitch, worked over a single thread of the canvas (see page 122 for stitching instructions).

Thread a needle with the outline colour and begin working the outline nearest to the centre of the chart. Knot the end of the thread and take the needle down through the canvas about 5 cm (2 in) from the start of the work. This thread can then be worked over at the back of the canvas as the embroidery progresses, and the knot can be cut off. Finish off threads in the same way by bringing each thread up 5 cm (2 in) from the embroidery and these will be worked in around one of the leaves. When the outline is complete fill in the colours as shown on the chart.

Use a length of wool in the needle not longer than 80 cm (32 in). If the thread is too long, it becomes worn and thin as you work and will not cover the canvas properly.

The background of the original embroidery in Hardwick Hall has horizontal bands of slightly different shades of colour, maybe due to changes in the natural dyes used. To achieve this effect today, mix several different shades of the same colour together in the needle at random, and work straight lines of tent stitch across the canvas.

Further suggestions

1 For a handsome evening bag, mix gold threads in the needle with stranded cotton or silk threads. Madeira Metallic threads would be suitable, using short lengths at a time. It must be noted, however, that stranded cottons and silks do not wear as well as wool.

2 This lovely leaf design would look wonderful in cross stitch as a rug on a coarse 10 stitches to 2.5 cm (1 in) canvas.

The design of oak leaves can be
used as a repeating pattern. This
plan, showing the chart from pages
48 and 49 repeated and joined up,
illustrates how the chart can be
adapted for this purpose.

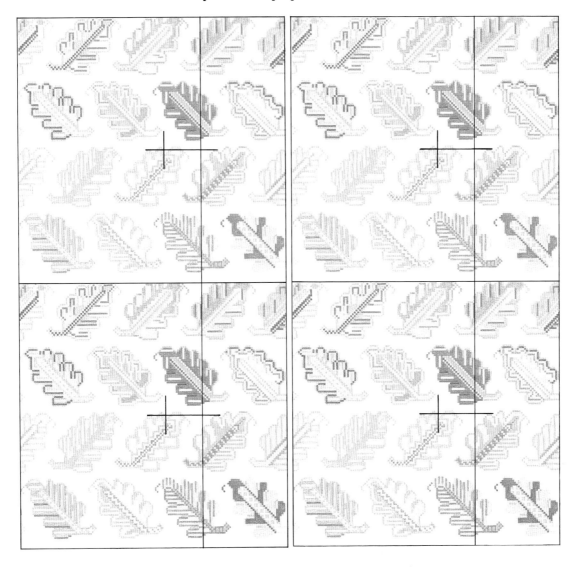

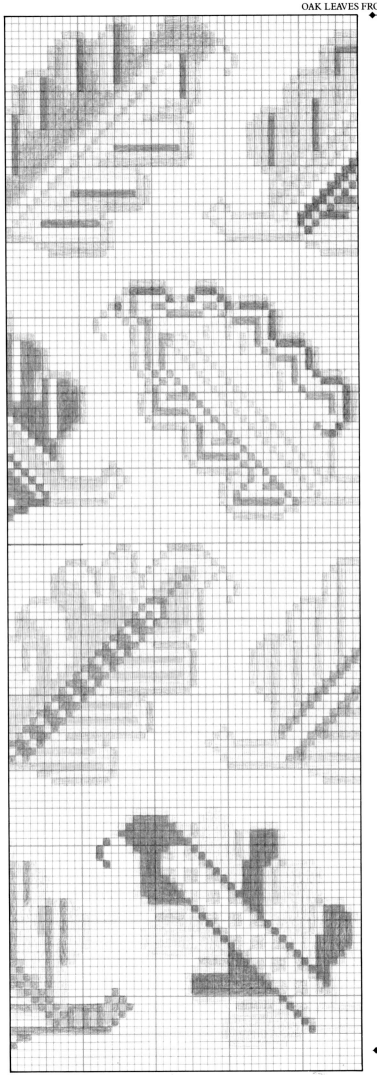

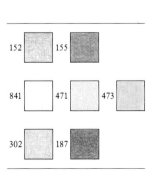

152 | 155

841 | 471 | 473

302 | 187

Bradford Table Carpet

◇

A detail from the Bradford table carpet, worked in silk on linen canvas in tent stitch, with some details in stem, long and short stitches. There are 400 stitches to the square inch and twenty-three colours. The whole piece measures 4m (13 ft) long and 1.75m (5 ft 9 in) wide. It was worked at sometime between 1605 and 1615 and was the property of the Earls of Bradford, after whom it is called although it does not include any heraldry connected with them. It may well have been made in a professional workshop for sale on the open market rather than being commissioned.

The centre or 'field' is filled with a repeating pattern of a vine, typical of this kind of work, although fields often also included coats of arms and scenes of hunting or of nature inserted in roundels or cartouches. Around the edge there is a series of pictures depicting man's evolution from a naked savage living in a tree house, through scenes of working people, including a milkmaid, huntsman and this miller, to the wealthy outside a palace designed in the latest architectural style. There are also a finely dressed courting couple and a married couple accompanied by their dog, which sits with his front paws crossed to show his owners' fidelity to one another. These scenes are typical of the philosophy of the period and there are some whose imagery we cannot fully understand today even though they provide a useful insight into seventeenth-century social history. The drawing of the figures and landscape is bold and quite detailed, although the scenes lack perspective and scale.

Table carpets were used in England until well into the seventeenth century and much later in Holland. During the first quarter of the seventeenth century carpets started to be used on the floor and the table was covered with a lighter weight cloth.

INSTRUCTIONS

The Bradford table carpet is an excellent picture of the social history of the late sixteenth century. This small section gives us an insight into the dress, architecture and countryside of the time. As this design is definitely 'one way up', it would be best reproduced as a picture, or possibly a cushion.

The original canvas used for the table carpet was 400 stitches to 2.5 cm (1 in), and the embroidery was worked in wool and silk. Because the canvas was so fine, the detail shown in the picture is very accurate. Modern silk threads are too bright to reproduce the original work well, so all wool threads have been chosen for this project as they are more mellow in appearance.

Materials

Good quality single canvas 18 stitches to 2.5 cm (1 in) (see page 120 for canvas). You will need 52.5 x 26.5 cm (21 x 10½ in) of canvas. Allow 7.5 cm (3 in) all around for making up. If you only want to work up part of the design see page 123 for adapting a chart.

For a really fine embroidery use a single German peach canvas, 22 stitches to 2.5 cm (1 in).

Use one or two strands of Appleton crewel wool in the needle depending on your tension. Practise a small area first to see which is sufficient to cover the canvas. If you use three strands remember to allow extra yarn.

The quantities of wool given below are approximate and will vary from person to person. It is important to buy the background wool in hanks, rather than skeins, and that each hank is from the same dye lot. The dye varies from lot to lot

and any change will show up in the background. If you do need to buy a second quantity mix the old batch with the new.

One skein of 121, 123, 126, 185, 186, 202, 203, 292, 472, 473, 474, 642, 692, 693, 705, 764, 954 and 993; half a hank of 124, 151, 184, 187, 291, 297, 305, 325, 328, 765, 766, 767, and 963; six skeins of 701, 763, 851, 961 and one hank of 181.

If you wish to use more wool the general rule is that one hank will cover an area of 15 x 15 cm (6 x 6 in).

Size 20 tapestry needles for size 18 canvas; size 22 needles for size 22 canvas. Use a needle which will take the correct number of threads without damaging them, and which will not distort the canvas when stitching.

Method of working

Fold the canvas in half both ways to find the centre. Mark the folds with a hard pencil or tacking stitches. A small, square peg frame would be best for this piece of work (see page 121); it could also be worked in a ring frame, but it must be nice and tight.

Match your threads to the colour chart key and number if necessary. Find the centre of the chart. Each coloured square on the chart represents one tent stitch, worked over a single thread of the canvas (see page 122 for stitching instructions).

Thread a needle with the colour used at the centre of the chart. Knot the end of the thread and take the needle down through the canvas about 5 cm (2 in) from the start of the work. This thread can then be worked over at the back of the canvas as the embroidery progresses, and the knot can be cut off. Finish off threads in the same way by bringing each thread up 5 cm (2 in) from the embroidery and these will be worked in.

Use a length of wool in the needle not longer than 80 cm (32 in). If the thread is too long, it becomes worn and thin as you work and will not cover the canvas properly.

Stitch outwards from the centre of the design. Complete the design before working the background up to it.

Further suggestions

1 Work the whole design in stranded cottons if you do not mind it looking brighter than the original and not quite as subtle as in wool. (Please note that stranded cottons and silks do not wear as well as silk)

2 Add silk or cotton threads to highlight features of the design.

PAGE 54   PAGE 56   PAGE 59   PAGE 60

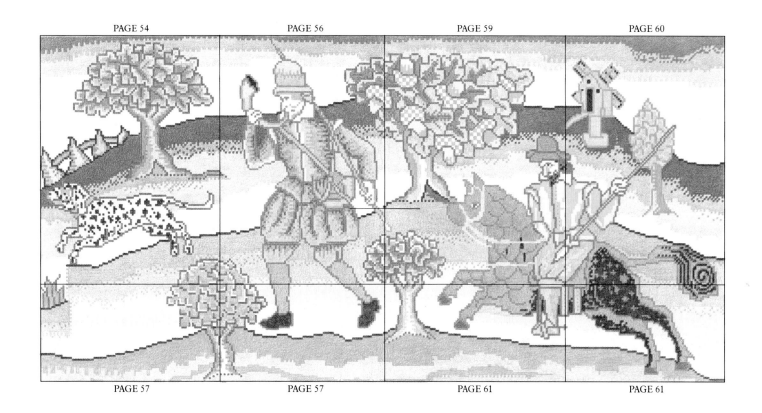

PAGE 57   PAGE 57   PAGE 61   PAGE 61

The plan shows the complete chart and the page numbers on which each section of the chart appears. The centre of the chart is shown here. If you only wish to work up a detail however —the huntsman, for example —you will have to locate the centre of that particular section.

▷ PAGE 56

PAGE 57 ▽

Please note: because of the large number of subtle tones in this design some of the colours on the chart have been used to signify more than one shade of wool. Therefore, the colours for each separate element of the design have been listed individually in the key. Each time you begin a new element of the design it is essential to refer to the key for the relevant wool numbers.

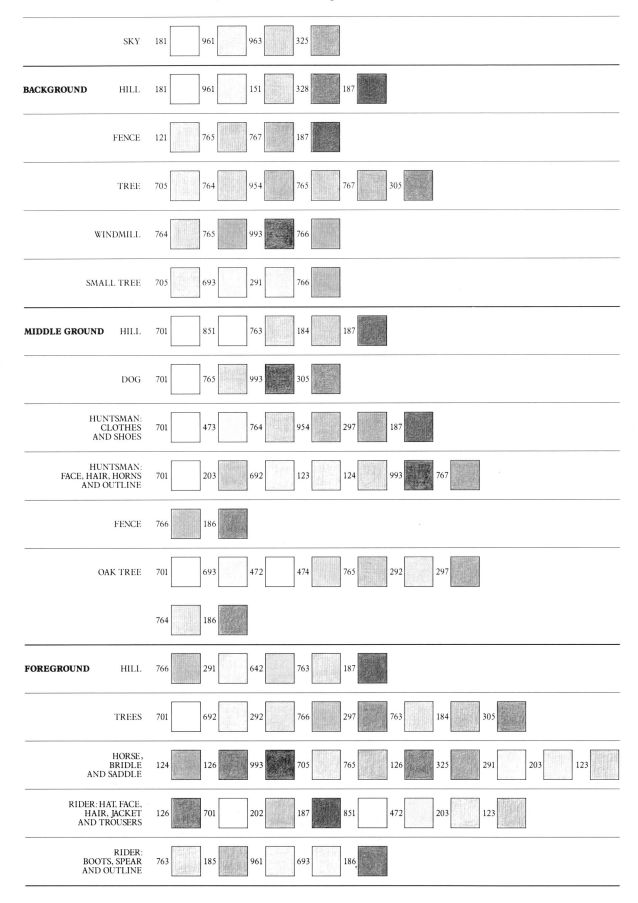

	SKY	181		961		963		325										
BACKGROUND	HILL	181		961		151		328		187								
	FENCE	121		765		767		187										
	TREE	705		764		954		765		767		305						
	WINDMILL	764		765		993		766										
	SMALL TREE	705		693		291		766										
MIDDLE GROUND	HILL	701		851		763		184		187								
	DOG	701		765		993		305										
	HUNTSMAN: CLOTHES AND SHOES	701		473		764		954		297		187						
	HUNTSMAN: FACE, HAIR, HORNS AND OUTLINE	701		203		692		123		124		993		767				
	FENCE	766		186														
	OAK TREE	701		693		472		474		765		292		297				
		764		186														
FOREGROUND	HILL	766		291		642		763		187								
	TREES	701		692		292		766		297		763		184		305		
	HORSE, BRIDLE AND SADDLE	124		126		993		705		765		126		325		291		203		123
	RIDER: HAT, FACE, HAIR, JACKET AND TROUSERS	126		701		202		187		851		472		203		123		
	RIDER: BOOTS, SPEAR AND OUTLINE	763		185		961		693		186								

◁ PAGE
54

▷ PAGE
59

PAGE 57 ▽

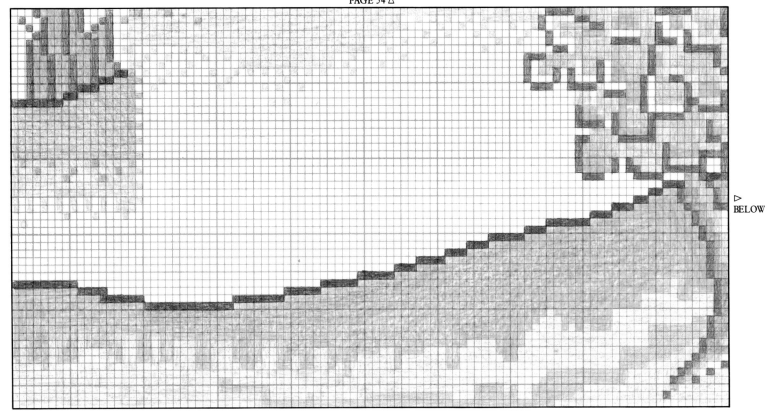

▷
BELOW

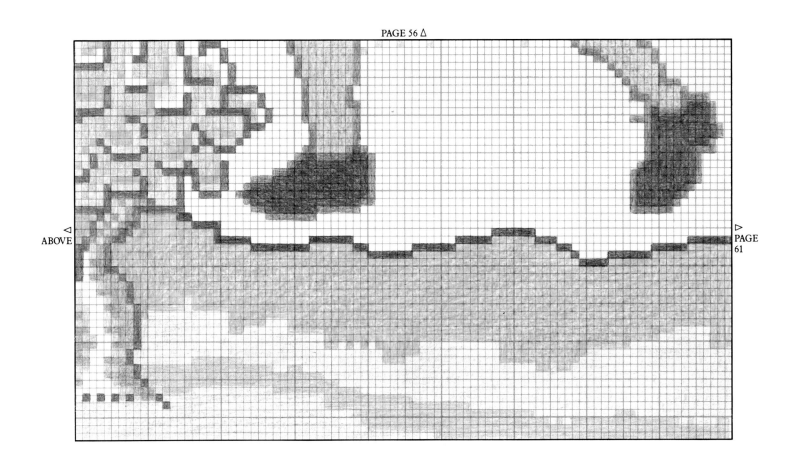

◁
ABOVE

▷
PAGE
61

Please note: because of the large number of subtle tones in this design some of the colours on the chart have been used to signify more than one shade of wool. Therefore, the colours for each separate element of the design have been listed individually in the key. Each time you begin a new element of the design it is essential to refer to the key for the relevant wool numbers.

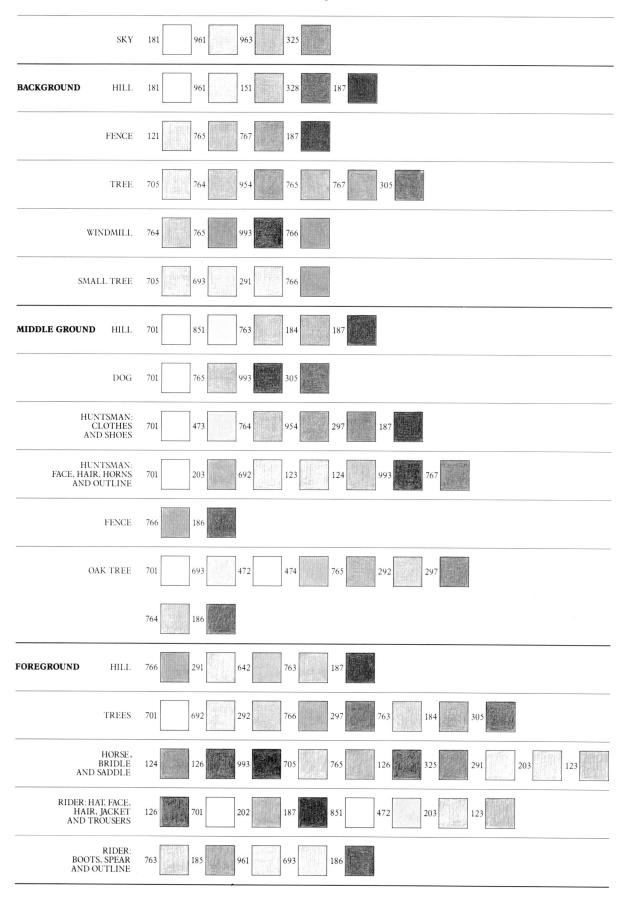

SKY 181 961 963 325

BACKGROUND HILL 181 961 151 328 187

FENCE 121 765 767 187

TREE 705 764 954 765 767 305

WINDMILL 764 765 993 766

SMALL TREE 705 693 291 766

MIDDLE GROUND HILL 701 851 763 184 187

DOG 701 765 993 305

HUNTSMAN: CLOTHES AND SHOES 701 473 764 954 297 187

HUNTSMAN: FACE, HAIR, HORNS AND OUTLINE 701 203 692 123 124 993 767

FENCE 766 186

OAK TREE 701 693 472 474 765 292 297

764 186

FOREGROUND HILL 766 291 642 763 187

TREES 701 692 292 766 297 763 184 305

HORSE, BRIDLE AND SADDLE 124 126 993 705 765 126 325 291 203 123

RIDER: HAT, FACE, HAIR, JACKET AND TROUSERS 126 701 202 187 851 472 203 123

RIDER: BOOTS, SPEAR AND OUTLINE 763 185 961 693 186

◁
PAGE
56

▷
PAGE
60

PAGE 61 ▽

◁
PAGE
59

PAGE 61 ▽

PAGE 59 △

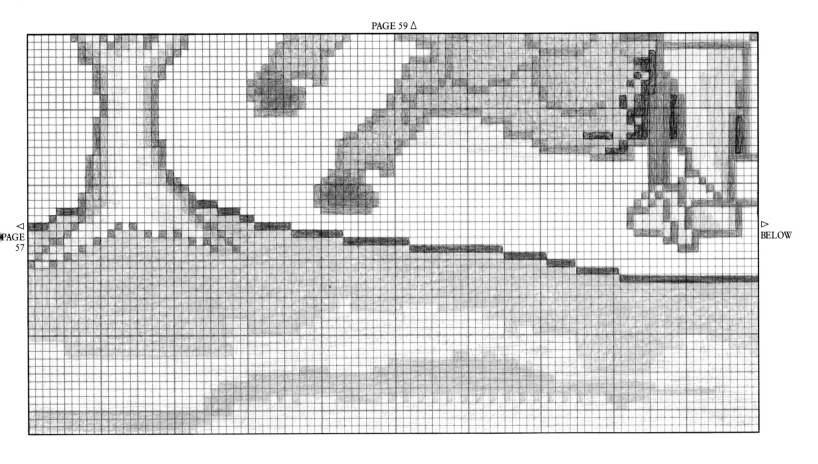

PAGE 57

BELOW

PAGE 60 △

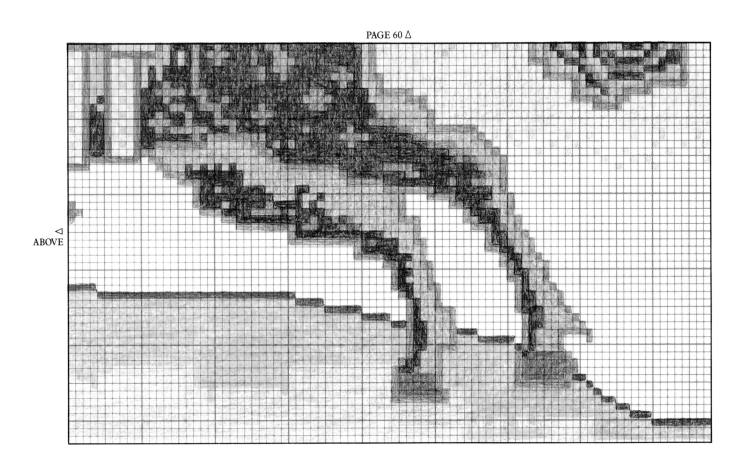

ABOVE

PAGE 59 △

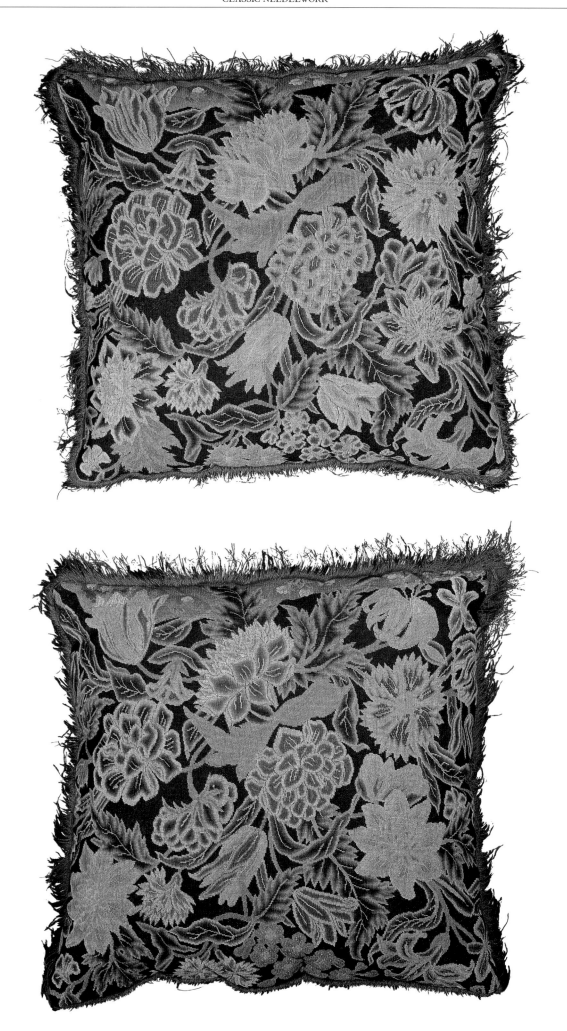

Queen Anne Cushion Covers

◇

A cushion cover from the early eighteenth century, which has been cut from a larger piece of embroidery. The large scale of the flowers suggests that it may have come from a set of panels intended as wall hangings or for a screen. Several such sets are known from this period.

Vivid exotic flowers, shown as here against a black background, are reminiscent of Dutch flower painting, while a bright yellow colour was very fashionable in the eighteenth century for both dress and furnishing fabrics. The flowers grow from mounds of earth at the base of the design, in a way typical of the first half of the eighteenth century, when many patterns were inspired by the Indian painted cloths or 'Chintz' being imported into Europe. Such designs were also fashionable for other types of embroidery and crewel work and were worked in different scales for use on dress as well as furnishing fabrics.

It is the mixture of styles and the bright yellow colour against a black ground in this piece which make it typically European, however. In Europe both amateur embroiderers and professional embroidery workshops often copied 'Indian' designs, some of which did not actually come from India but were imported from other eastern countries through trading companies operating in India. Such western versions of Chinese art became known as 'Chinoiserie'.

INSTRUCTIONS

The bold designs on these cushions would also be suitable for chair seats or stool tops. (see page 123 for instructions on making a template).

(see page 123 for instructions on making a template).

Materials

Single canvas, 16 stitches to 2.5 cm (1 in). You will need 41 x 41 cm (16¼ x 16¼ in) of canvas. Allow an extra 7.5 cm (3 in) of canvas all round for making up.

Use two or three strands of Appleton crewel wool in the needle. Practise a small area first to see if this is sufficient to cover the canvas. You may need to use three strands, in which case allow extra yarn.

The quantities of wool given below are approximate and will vary from person to person. It is important to buy the background wool in hanks, rather than skeins, and that each hank is from the same dye lot as any change will show up on the background. If you do need to buy a second quantity mix the old batch with the new.

One skein of 151, 152, 154, 155, 157, 183, 202, 203, 205, 207, 292, 295, 296, 326, 475, 641, 643, and 697; two skeins of 159, 472, 702, 841 and 881; four skeins of 473 and 474 and one hank of 588 (brown) or 993 (black) for the background, depending upon whether you would like this to be brown or black.

If you wish to use more wool, the general rule is that one hank will cover an area of 15 x 15 cm (6 x 6 in).

Size 20/22 tapestry needles.

Method of working

Fold the canvas in half twice to find the centre. Mark the folds with a hard pencil or tacking stitches. If you like to work with a frame, see page 121.

Match your threads to the colour chart key and number if necessary. Find the centre of the chart. Each coloured square on the chart represents one tent stitch, worked over a single thread of the canvas (see page 122 for stitching instructions).

Thread a needle with the colour used at the centre of the chart. Knot the end of the thread and take the needle down through the canvas about 5 cm (2 in) from the start of the work. This thread can then be worked over at the back of the canvas as the embroidery progresses, and the knot can be cut off. Finish off threads in the same way by bringing each thread up 5 cm (2 in) from the embroidery. These will be worked in.

Use a length of wool in the needle not longer than 80 cm (32 in). If the thread is too long, it becomes worn and thin as you work and will not cover the canvas properly.

Stitch outwards from the centre of the design. Complete the design before working the background up to it.

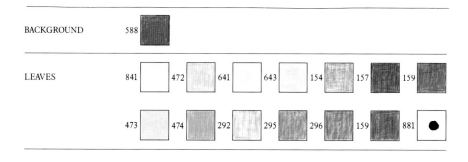

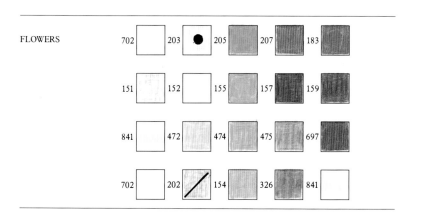

Further suggestions

1 Work background in a different stitch. Chequer stitch (see page 122) would look good worked up to the fine tent stitch flowers.

2 If the design is to be used on upholstery or cushions, it would not be advisable to use stranded threads to highlight the work, as they will not wear as well as wool.

The plan (right) shows the complete chart and indicates the page numbers on which each section of the chart appears. The piece should be worked from the centre outwards. A black keyline marks this central area which is reproduced as a full-size chart detail above. The same black keyline also indentifies this area on each section of the chart (pages 66 - 69).

PAGE 66   PAGE 67

PAGE 68   PAGE 69

Please note: many subtle shades are used
in the chart, therefore the colours for each
separate element of the design have been
listed individually in the key.

PAGE 68 ▽

The central area within the black keyline
is duplicated on page 65.

PAGE 69 ▽

Please note: many subtle shades are used
in the chart, therefore the colours for each
separate element of the design have been
listed individually in the key.

△

The central area within the black keyline
is duplicated on·page 65.

Shepherdess

A panel from an early eighteenth-century English chair, worked in wool and silk on canvas.

Sets of chairs were often upholstered in needlework with a series of pictures taken from a set of engravings. This pastoral scene of a shepherdess is simpler than many and may have been taken from an illustration to a Greek myth or fable. The drawing and design have a lightness and fantasy to them, in keeping with the fashion for rococo decoration.

Although this particular panel may well have been worked for a single chair, possibly by an amateur, whole sets for chairs and double-seat sofas are also known. Each seat from a set of perhaps eight chairs and two sofas would be decorated with a different picture, allowing a complete series of prints from a book to be used. Sometimes the original prints were altered by the embroiderer but many of those that survive are quite faithful reproductions, with only a few details changed. The choice of print was considered to show that the embroiderer had taste and knew what was fashionable, while the complexity of the picture demonstrated her skill in transferring the image to the embroidery. Many of the prints chosen were very popular ones by well-known illustrators.

Suites of chairs and sofas were placed around the walls of reception rooms and brought forward into the room by the servants only when they were required for sitting on. They were therefore intended in many cases to be objects of admiration as much as practical pieces of furniture.

INSTRUCTIONS

This charming design would make a very nice cushion cover or, of course, a picture as it is very much a 'one way up' design'.

Materials

Single canvas, 16 stitches to 2.5 cm (1 in). You will need 45 x 39 cm (18 x 15½ in) of canvas. Allow an extra 7.5 cm (3 in) all around for making up.

Single canvas, 18 or 22 stitches to 2.5 cm (1 in) can be used to give a fine look similar to the original pieces of work.

Use two or three strands of Appleton crewel wool in the needle depending on your tension. Practise a small area first to see which is sufficient to cover the canvas. If you use three strands allow extra yarn.

The quantities of wool given below are approximate and will vary from person to person. It is important to buy the background wool in hanks, rather than skeins, and that each hank is from the same dye lot. The dye varies slightly from lot to lot and any change will show up on the background. If you do need to buy a second quantity then you will need to mix the old batch with the new.

One skein of 186, 202, 323 and 647; two skeins of 203, 643, 692 and 704; three skeins of 205, 694 and 993; four skeins of 207 and 764; one hank of 325 and 693; one and a half hanks of 328 and three hanks of 701 for the background areas.

If you wish to use more wool the general rule is that one hank will cover an area of 15 x 15 cm (6 x 6 in).

Size 20 or 22 tapestry needles for 16- and 18-thread canvas; size 22 or 24 for 22-thread canvas. Use a needle which will take the correct number of threads without damaging them, and which will not distort the canvas when stitching.

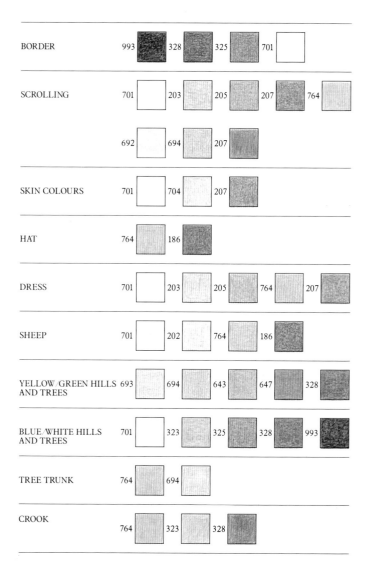

Please note: many subtle shades are used in the chart, therefore the colours for each separate element of the design have been listed individually in the key.

Opposite: the plan shows the complete chart and page numbers on which each section of the chart appears. The centre of the chart is shown here.

Method of working

Fold the canvas in half twice to find the centre. Mark the folds with a hard pencil or tacking stitches. A square peg frame is best for this piece of work or, failing that, a deep-sided ring frame (see page 121).

Match your threads to the colour chart key and number if necessary. Find the centre of the chart. Each coloured square on the chart represents one tent stitch, worked over a single thread of the canvas (see page 122 for stitching instructions).

Thread a needle with the colour used at the centre of the chart. Knot the end of the thread and take the needle down through the canvas about 5 cm (2 in) from the start of the work. This thread can then be worked over at the back of the canvas as the embroidery progresses, and the knot can be cut off. Finish off threads in the same way by bringing each thread up 5 cm (2 in) from the embroidery. These will be worked in.

Use a length of wool in the needle not longer than 80 cm (32 in). If the thread is too long, it becomes worn and thin as you work and will not cover the canvas properly.

Stitch outwards from the centre of the design. Complete the design before working the background up to it.

Further suggestions

1 Substitute silk or stranded cotton threads for working the figure of the shepherdess. These threads will not wear as well as wool, but would be suitable for a picture.

2 After working the sheep, add small French knots to the tent stitch to give them a woolly appearance.

PAGE 74   PAGE 75   PAGE 78

PAGE 76   PAGE 77   PAGE 79

PAGE 76 ▽

PAGE
78

PAGE 77 ▽

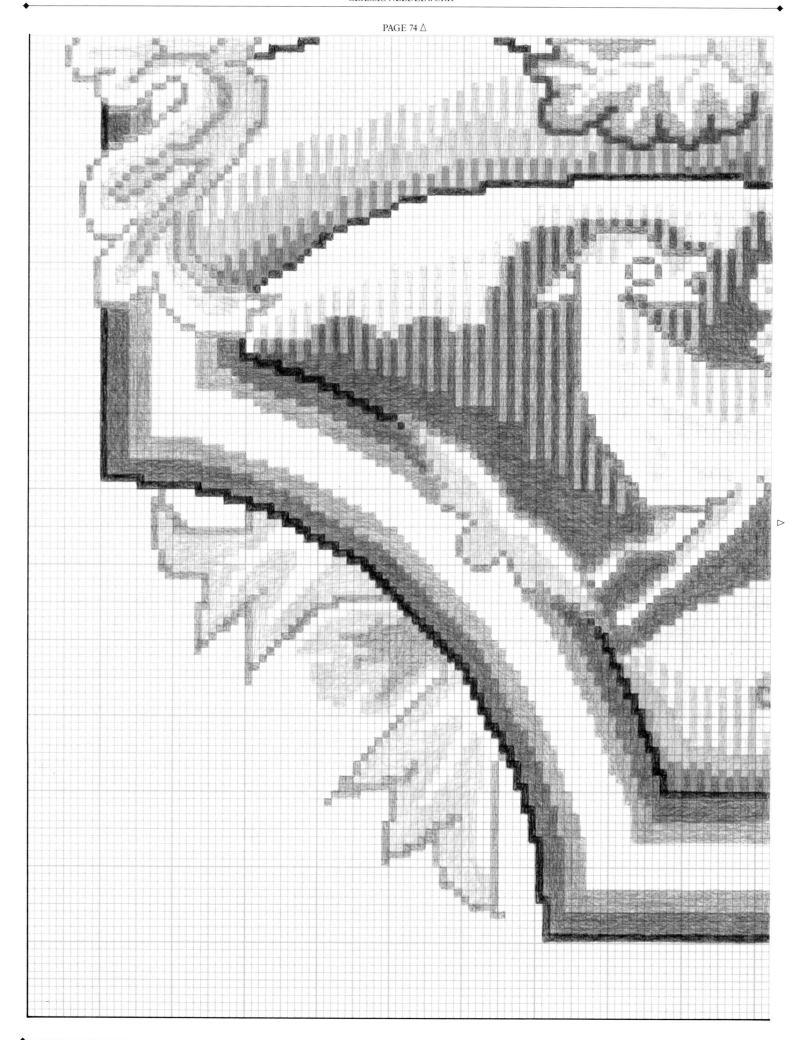

PAGE 75 △

△

▷
PAGE
79

PAGE 75 △

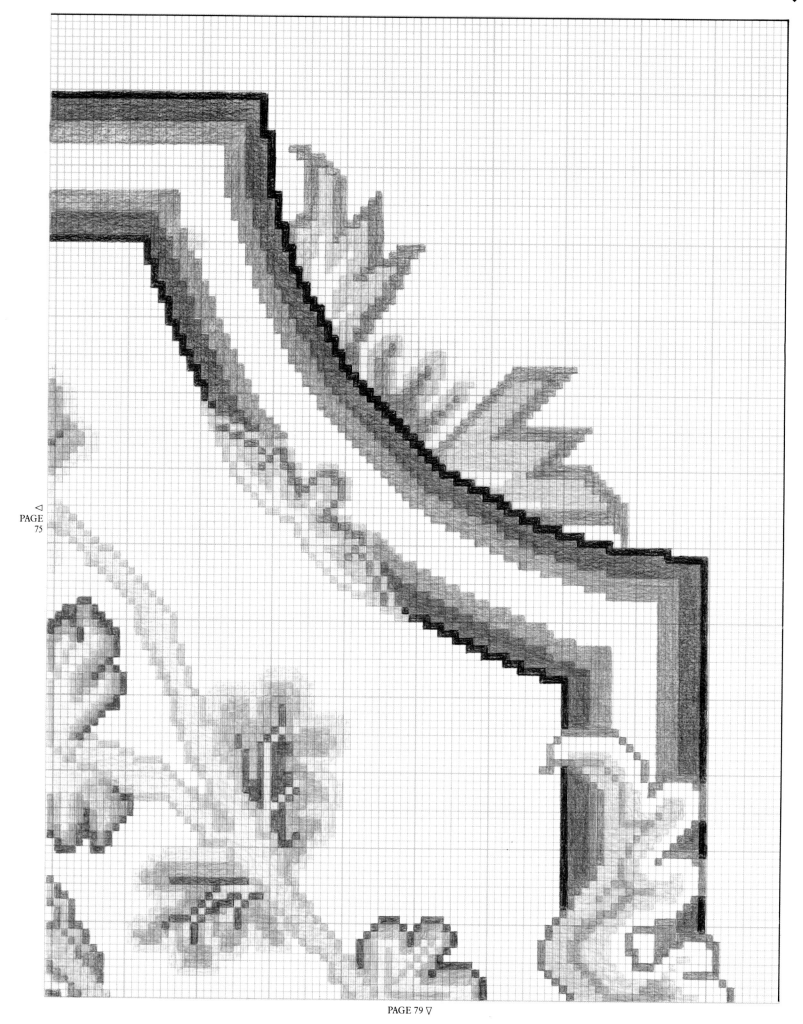

◁
PAGE
75

PAGE 79 ▽

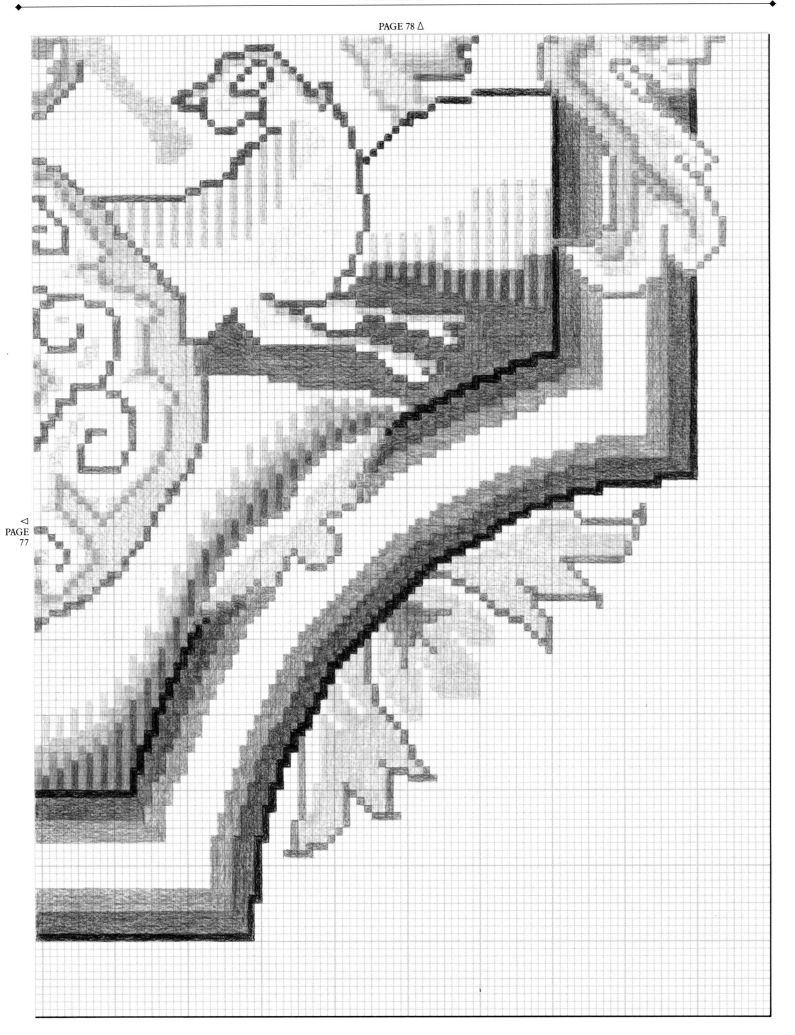

△
PAGE
77

American Wing Armchair

An American wing armchair which has been upholstered in needlework wool embroidery, *circa* 1720s.

The yards of upholstery required for this chair may well have been worked in a professional workshop. A loose squab cushion, also covered in canvas work, could have been used with it. Its elegant proportions are ideally suited to the fashionable North American interior of this period.

Repeating patterns of this sort were quick to work and were very much in vogue in the first half of the eighteenth century, although designs never entirely went out of fashion, any more than did the wing armchair itself, which was first introduced in the 1660s. There is a great range of colour in this piece of needlework, varying from deep subtle tones to much brighter shades, which reflect the fashion for more vivid tones at this period.

Writing much later, in 1906, Mrs Grace Christie commented on the use of repeating patterns in canvas work for chair covers. Well-known for her work on English medieval embroidery and for her contribution to the teaching of needlework at the beginning of this century, she commended such designs as pleasant and satisfactory. Although eighteenth-century design enjoyed a fashionable revival during the late nineteenth and early twentieth centuries, it did not generally appeal to the artists of the time. Grace Christie herself considered the floral patterns on eighteenth century textiles too brightly coloured and naturalistic, although a relatively muted design such as this would have pleased her and her fellow artists and historians far more.

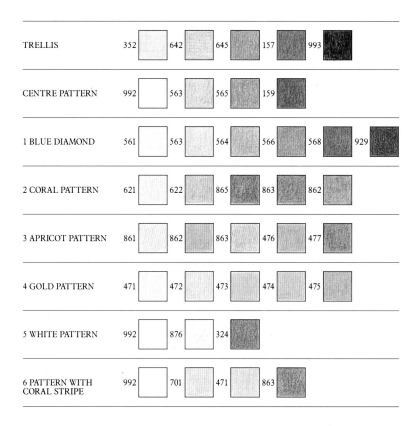

TRELLIS	352		642		645		157		993	
CENTRE PATTERN	992		563		565		159			
1 BLUE DIAMOND	561		563		564		566		568	929
2 CORAL PATTERN	621		622		865		863		862	
3 APRICOT PATTERN	861		862		863		476		477	
4 GOLD PATTERN	471		472		473		474		475	
5 WHITE PATTERN	992		876		324					
6 PATTERN WITH CORAL STRIPE	992		701		471		863			

INSTRUCTIONS

This wonderful chair is a real treasure, completely covered in a Florentine repeat pattern. Florentine embroidery is most suitable for furnishings and this design could be used on chair seats, stool tops and cushions (see page 123 for instructions on making a template).

If you are really ambitious, there is nothing to stop you covering your own chair. You would need to make a template of the various parts of the chair to be covered (see page 123). If the chair is of complex construction, it would be best to ask an upholsterer to do it for you. Because this is a comparatively large design, you will need to use as fine a canvas as possible to get a reasonable number of repeats.

Materials

Single canvas, 18 stitches to 2.5 cm (1 in). The size of canvas will obviously vary according to how you plan to use the project (see page 124 for adapting a chart). The size of one diamond is 15 x 11.5 cm (6 x $4\frac{1}{2}$ in). Allow an extra 7.5 cm (3 in) all around for making up.

Use two strands of Appleton crewel wool in the needle. Practise a small area first to see if this is sufficient to cover the canvas. You may need to use three strands, in which case allow extra yarn.

The quantities of wool required for this project will depend on how you choose to use the design. The general rule to calculate the amount of wool you need is that one hank will cover an area of 15 x 15 cm (6 x 6 in).

Size 22 tapestry needles.

The design on the chair comprises a repeating diamond pattern, with many slight variations in the colours of the diamonds. Six colour schemes to create this repeating pattern are illustrated on the charts on pages 84-85. If you wish to cover a large area you should first devise a repeating pattern for some, or all, of these individual colour schemes.

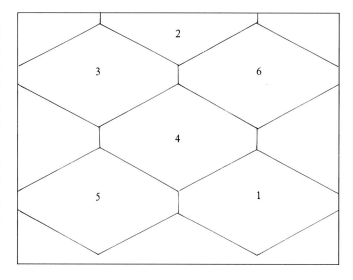

The plan shows the complete chart and the page numbers on which they appear.

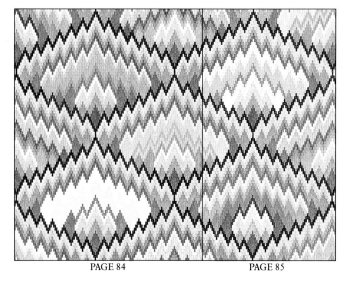

PAGE 84   PAGE 85

Method of working

Fold the canvas in half both ways to find the centre. Mark the folds with a hard pencil or tacking stitches. Ideally use a square peg frame to work the embroidery, or a deep-sided ring frame (see page 121).

Match your threads to the colour chart key and number if necessary. Thread up a range of colours in several needles to speed up the work. Find the centre of the chart, then locate the nearest outline stitch. Each stitch is a straight stitch worked over four threads of canvas.

Thread a needle with the outline colour and work round the diamond shape (see page 122 for stitching instructions). To start, knot the end of the thread and take the needle down through the canvas about 5 cm (2 in) from the start of the work. This thread can then be worked over at the back of the canvas as the embroidery progresses, and the knot can be cut off. Finish off threads in the same way by bringing each thread up 5 cm (2 in) from the embroidery and these will be worked in.

Use a length of wool in the needle not longer than 80 cm (32 in). If the thread is too long, it becomes worn and thin as you work and will not cover the canvas properly.

Work each diamond shape in turn, changing colour in each row if appropriate.

Further suggestions

1 Work the Florentine pattern on a large bag, using a good quality canvas, 22 stitches to 2.5 cm (1 in). Substitute stranded cotton or silk threads for some of the paler shades to highlight the design. (These threads are not suitable for furnishings because they are not as hard-wearing as wool.)

Below: This repeating pattern has been worked on a canvas of 16 stitches to 2.5 cm (1 in).

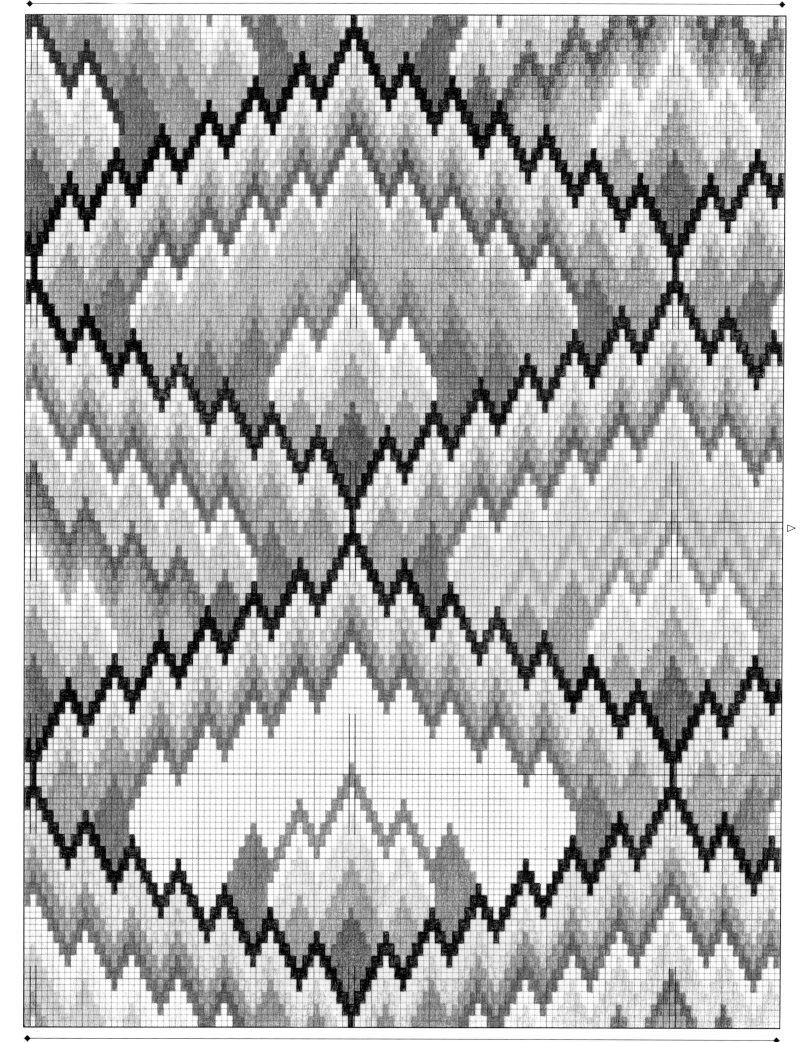

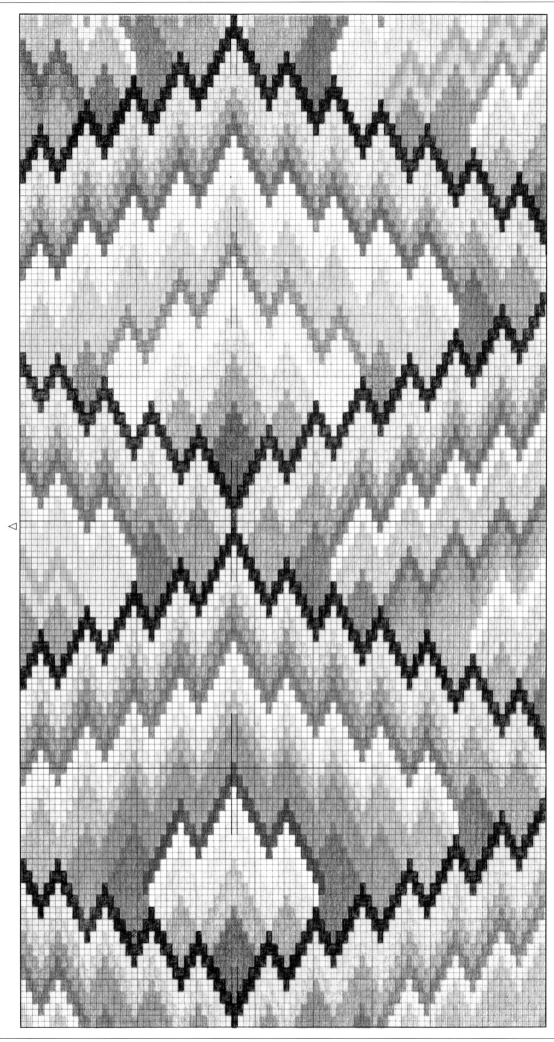

Please note: the key on page 82 shows the colour schemes for each diamond. The colours are arranged in order working from the outside of each diamond inwards to the centre.

One Florentine stitch is represented on the chart by four coloured squares. The black keylines mark the centre of each diamond and the central stitch where the diamonds join.

Eighteenth-century Needlecase

—— ◇ ——

A needlecase dated 1749, which could be rolled up, tied and kept in a work box.

The outside is worked with a small repeating pattern in a rich combination of colours. Inside there is canvas work of a quite different design, again very small in scale but depicting flowers, birds and dogs on a dark ground. The motifs may possibly have been taken directly from a sampler. There are five pockets for holding needlework tools, and leaves of red flannel for needles. Each of the pockets is lined with silk.

During the eighteenth century a number of small household items and dress accessories were decorated with canvas work, based in many cases on repeating patterns and small, simple motifs. Pocket books, card cases and sewing cases were all fashionable. Such intimate items were usually worked by amateurs and sometimes given as presents. The initials and dates of the embroiderer or the owner are often included in the design. Canvas work in similar designs was also used for Bible covers. One from New England includes the inscription 'Holy Bible Aaron Chew his book May 4 1797'.

A larger version of the needlecase took the form of a wall pocket, which was very popular in the United States and some European countries. The back, which hung against the wall, was not necessarily decorative, but the front pockets offered a splendid opportunity for needleworkers to demonstrate their skill. Canvas work embroidery formed a decorative textile that was strong enough to hold a variety of small objects.

INSTRUCTIONS

This beautiful little needlecase is worked on a very fine-mesh background in silk thread. If you want to be authentic, silk-mesh canvas, 38 stitches to 2.5 cm (1 in), would give a result similar to the original embroidery.

The design has been adapted so that the project can be worked on a canvas which will be easier on the eyes, but still be a suitable size for a needlecase.

Materials

Single canvas, 24 stitches to 2.5 cm (1 in). For the area shown on the chart you will need 8 x 35 cm (3 x 14 in). Allow an extra 7.5 cm (3 in) all around for making up.

Use two threads of Appleton crewel wool in the needle. Practise a small area first to see if this is sufficient to cover the canvas.

The quantities of wool given below are approximate and will vary from person to person. If you wish to use more wool the general rule is that one hank will cover an area of 15 x 15 cm (6 x 6 in).

One skein of 149, 184, 221, 253, 323, 405, 407, 472, 542, 544, 561, 562, 564, 695, 712, 755, 757, 841, 842 and 881 and two skeins of 403 and 935.

Size 20 or 22 tapestry needles for 16- and 18-thread canvas; size 24 for a 24-thread canvas. Use a needle which will take the correct number of threads without damaging them, and which will not distort the canvas when stitching.

Method of working

Fold the canvas in half twice to find the centre. Mark the folds with a hard pencil or tacking stitches. Ideally use a square peg frame to work the embroidery, or a deep-sided ring frame, with the canvas very tight (see page 121).

Match your threads to the colour chart key and number if necessary. Thread up a range of colours in several needles to speed up the work.

Find the centre of the chart, then locate the nearest outline stitch. Each stitch is a straight stitch worked over four threads of canvas.

Thread a needle with the outline colour and work round the diamond (see page 122 for stitching instructions). To start, knot the end of the thread and take the needle down through the canvas about 5 cm (2 in) from the start of the work. This thread can then be worked over at the back of the canvas as the embroidery progresses, and the knot can be cut off. Finish off threads in the same way by bringing each thread up 5 cm (2 in) from the embroidery and these will be worked in.

Use a length of thread in the needle not longer than 80 cm (32 in). If the thread is too long, it becomes worn and thin as you work and will not cover the canvas properly.

Work in rows to complete each outline shape. Then work each colour following the outline until you reach the centre.

Further suggestions

1 Add highlights to the embroidery by using stranded cotton or silk for the paler shades.

2 Work the Florentine design on a cushion, using canvas size 16 stitches to 2.5 cm (1 in) and adapting the chart.

3 Make a rich, Renaissance-style waist-coat to co-ordinate with a wide range of plain colours. Use stranded cotton or silk threads and a fine canvas, 16, 18 or 22 stitches to 2.5 cm (1 in).

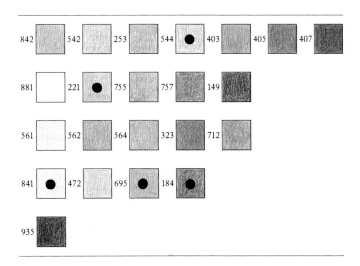

The original needlecase was worked on
a very fine mesh canvas. In order for the
design to work on a larger canvas, but
still be a suitable size for a needlecase,
only half the pattern has been charted.
If you should wish to use this design
as a basis for a larger repeating pattern
you can adapt the chart and work the
pattern horizontally as well as vertically.

PAGE
88

PAGE
89

PAGE 89 ▽

Please note: one Florentine stitch is represented on the chart by four coloured squares. The black keylines mark the centre of each diamond and the central stitch where the diamonds join.

Eighteenth-century Floral
Seat Cover

The centre panel from a chair seat of the mid-eighteenth century. The central spray of flowers on a cream ground is surrounded by an elaborate pattern of intertwining flowers and curving lines worked in bright colours on a plain blue ground. It is possible that this part was stitched at a later date, as the chair seat was left unfinished.

By the 1730s there was more naturalism in flower drawing. Not only had the production of pattern books increased; there were also publications to help amateur needle-workers improve their drawing technique so that they could design or at any rate redraw motifs for themselves. By the late eighteenth century ladies' magazines were well established and advice and patterns for embroidery could easily be obtained.

The central motif in this chair seat could also have been used for other kinds of furniture, such as a pole screen. Placed between the fire and a lady's face, the screen was moved up and down the pole to suit the sitter's height. On days when a fire was not required, the pole screen became another decorative item in the room. Small pieces of occasional furniture of this type were very much a part of the fashionable interior in the mid-eighteenth century.

INSTRUCTIONS

This colourful design was originally worked on a linen background. The bunch of flowers in the centre was worked in tent stitch over one thread, and the border was worked over two threads. To get this effect today, we would use double canvas and split it for the finer stitch in the centre. However, we are only planning to work the centre motif with the border worked over one thread too, so it will be easier to use single canvas. Thread several needles with different colours to speed up the work.

This design would obviously be very suitable for a chair seat or stool top (see page 123 for instructions on making a template). It would equally well make a lovely cushion or fire screen.

This design has been worked on a canvas of 18 stitches to 2.5 cm (1 in)

Materials

Single canvas, 16 stitches to 2.5 cm (1 in). You will need 44.5 x 44.5 cm (17½ x 17½ in) of canvas. Allow an extra 7.5 cm (3 in) of canvas all around for making up.

Use two or three strands of Appleton crewel wool in the needle. Practise a small area first to see if this is sufficient to cover the canvas. You may need to use three strands, in which case allow extra yarn.

The quantities of wool given below are approximate and will vary from person to person. It is important to buy the background wool in hanks, rather than skeins, and that each hank is from the same dye lot. The dye varies slightly from lot to lot and any change will show up on the background. If you do need to buy a second quantity mix the old batch with the new.

You will require one skein of 153, 155, 158, 159, 208, 226, 251, 253, 254, 255, 311, 313, 315, 474, 475, 476, 478, 501A, 528, 602, 605, 701, 716, 841, 842 and 844; two skeins of 127, 208, 402, 403, 405, 407, 502, 603 and 715; four skeins of 503; two hanks of 744 and four hanks of 882 for the backgrounds.

If you wish to use more wool the general rule is that one hank will cover an area of 15 x 15 cm (6 x 6 in).

Size 20/22 tapestry needles.

Method of working

Fold your canvas in half twice to find the centre. Mark the folds with a hard pencil or with tacking stitches. Ideally use a square peg frame to work the embroidery (see page 121).

Match your threads to the colour chart key and number if necessary. Find the centre of the chart. Each coloured square on the chart represents one tent stitch, worked over a single thread of the canvas (see page 122 for stitching instructions).

Thread a needle with the colour used at the centre of the chart. Knot the end of this thread and take the needle down through the canvas 5 cm (2 in) from the start of the work. This thread will be worked over at the back of the canvas as the embroidery progresses, and the knot can be cut off. Finish off threads in the same way by bringing each thread up 5 cm (2 in) from the embroidery; these will be worked in.

Use a length of wool in the needle not longer than 80 cm (32 in). If the thread is too long, it becomes worn and thin as you work and will not cover the canvas properly.

Stitch outwards from the centre of the design. Complete the design before working the background up to it.

Further suggestions

1 If the design is to be made into a picture, use stranded cotton for some of the lightest shades, to highlight the work. Stranded cottons would not be suitable for a chair seat or stool top because they do not wear as well as wool.

2 Work the background in a different stitch. Choose one that will not overpower the dainty design. Any of the following stitches would be suitable: Hungarian stitch, chequer stitch, cashmere stitch, upright cross stitch or straight Gobelin stitch. (See page 122).

The plan shows the complete chart and the page numbers on which they appear.

PAGE 94   PAGE 95

PAGE 96   PAGE 97

Please note: many subtle shades are used
in the chart, therefore the colours for
each separate element of the design have
been listed individually in the key.

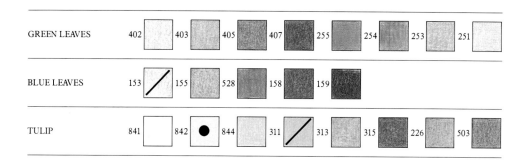

| GREEN LEAVES | 402 | | 403 | | 405 | | 407 | | 255 | | 254 | | 253 | | 251 | |

| BLUE LEAVES | 153 | | 155 | | 528 | | 158 | | 159 | |

| TULIP | 841 | | 842 | | 844 | | 311 | | 313 | | 315 | | 226 | | 503 | |

PAGE 96 ▽

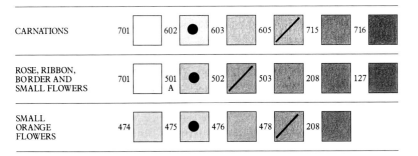

PAGE 97 ▽

PAGE 94 △

GREEN LEAVES	402		403		405		407		255		254		253		251	
BLUE LEAVES	153		155		528		158		159								
TULIP	841		842	●	844		311	/	313		315		226		503	

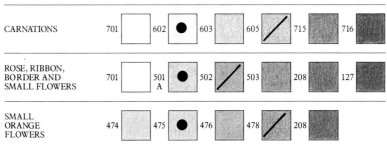

CARNATIONS	701		602	● 603	605	/ 715	716	
ROSE, RIBBON, BORDER AND SMALL FLOWERS	701		501 A	● 502	/ 503	208	127	
SMALL ORANGE FLOWERS	474		475	● 476	478	/ 208		

Florentine Repeating Pattern

—— ◇ ——

An English chair seat from the mid-eighteenth century. The linen has been embroidered in wool and silk in Florentine stitch which creates a softly blurred pattern. It is possible that it was used on a set of chairs with carved, wooden backs.

Needlework upholstery had become popular in the late seventeenth century. There are fine sets of chairs and sofas covered in this design in several country houses and there are references to furniture makers receiving orders for furniture upholstered in needle-work of the clients' own making. Sets of embroidered chair seats were also available from professional workshops.

Repeating patterns of this kind are sometimes known as 'flame' patterns and they vary endlessly, with colour and stitching combined to form a warm and interesting surface. The stitches used for flame patterns include Florentine, also known as punto fiamma, Hungarian point and bargello.

The design of diamonds and flowers relies very heavily on the use of subtle colour for effect. In places the darker tones form an optical illusion so that the centres of the diamonds appear to jump forward. A wide colour range has been chosen, combining dark rich shades with pastel ones. The pale blue ground, used for every other flower, helps to balance the light areas against the dark. In places the blue silk has worn away. The pinks are drawn with a certain amount of naturalism although they have been shaped to fit the overall design of diamonds.

During the eighteenth century there was an emphasis on achieving evenness of embroidery and interesting surface patterns, rather than on using different stitches to create a textured effect.

INSTRUCTIONS

Florentine patterns are mostly used to decorate cushions, chair seats, stools and so on. They can also be worked on a fine canvas, 22 stitches to 2.5 cm (1 in), and made into a bag.

Materials

Single canvas, 16 stitches to 2.5 cm (1 in). (If you use too coarse a canvas for Florentine work, the long stitches easily become caught and are liable to get pulled and will wear badly.) The size of the canvas will obviously vary according to how you plan to use the project (see page 123 for adapting a chart). Always allow an extra 7.5 cm (3 in) all around for making up.

Use two or three strands of Appleton crewel wool in the needle. Practise a small area first to see how many threads cover the canvas best. If you need to use three threads allow extra yarn.

The quantities of wool required for this project will depend on how you choose to use the design. The general rule to calculate the amount of wool you need is that one hank will cover an area of 15 x 15 cm (6 x 6 in).

It is important to remember that you should buy the background wool in hanks, rather than skeins, and that each hank is from the same dye lot. The dye varies slightly from lot to lot and any change will show up on the background. If you do need to buy a second quantity mix the old batch with the new.

Size 20/22 tapestry needles.

Method of working

Fold the canvas in half twice to find the centre. Mark the folds with a hard pencil or with tacking stitches. Ideally use a square slate frame to work the embroidery, or alternatively a deep-sided ring frame (see page 121).

Match your threads to the colour chart key and number if necessary. The chart can be worked so that there is either a diamond or a carnation at the centre of the pattern. Decide which way you would like to use the design. Find the centre of either the diamond or the carnation on the chart, then locate the nearest outline stitch. Each stitch is a straight stitch worked over four threads of canvas.

Thread a needle with the outline colour and work round the shape (see page 122 for stitching instructions). To start, knot the end of the thread and take the needle down through the canvas about 5 cm (2 in) from the start of the work. This thread can then be worked over at the back of the canvas as the embroidery progresses, and the knot can be cut off. Finish off threads in the same way by bringing each thread up 5 cm (2 in) from the embroidery and these will be worked in.

Use a length of thread in the needle not longer than 80 cm (32 in). If the thread is too long, it becomes worn and thin as you work and will not cover the canvas properly.

Work each colour by following the outline of the shape until you reach the centre of it.

Further suggestions

1 If the embroidery is to be made into a bag, work the lighter shades of the design in stranded cotton or shiny thread to high light the design. (These threads will not wear as well as wools, however.)

2 Work the whole of the carnation flower in stranded cotton. This would be suitable on a fine canvas, and for an article that will not have a lot of hard wear.

3 Work the diamond in the centre of the pattern in beads, again for an item which will not get a lot of wear.

BACKGROUND	705	876					
GOLD SHAPES	934	694	226	503	694	472	694
	705	159	832	252	694	705	
GREEN SHAPES	934	159	644	832	252	694	
	705	226	503	694	472	694	705
CARNATION	753	756	948	159	832	252	472

Please note: many subtle shades are used in the chart, therefore the colours for each separate element of the design have been listed individually in the key.

*The Florentine repeat pattern has been
worked on a canvas of 16 stitches to
2.5 cm (1 in). The needleworker has created
a brighter design, instead of the softer and
more muted effect of the original, by using
wool number 544 instead of 832.*

These two plans illustrate the charts of the diamond and the carnations joined together. The repeating pattern can be worked with either the carnations or the diamonds at the centre of the design.

Please note: the first vertical row of
stitches on the left-hand side of the chart
on the opposite page (105) is a repeat of
the last row of stitches on the right-hand
side of the chart on this page. However,
you need to work this row once only.

Please note: the white background areas
to the carnations should be worked in
pink, Appleton crewl wool 705, and blue,
Appleton crewel wool 876, alternately.

Posies

A pattern on graph paper, showing motifs for working in berlin wools.

While the particular flowers shown here have seasonal characteristics, motifs of this kind could have been combined and used in various ways and for different purposes. The origins of this pattern are unknown, but by the early nineteenth century the publication of patterns for wool work was a flourishing commercial business.

It seems that a Berlin publisher first produced patterns on graph paper in 1804, so as to create designs which would be simple to copy square by square onto canvas. The first patterns reproduced delicate floral designs, of the sort associated with the early nine-teenth century. Four craftsmen were originally involved in the production of the patterns, although this number was later reduced when colour printing came into more general use. The first craftsman made a master copy from the original painted picture or design; the second ruled it into squares and marked where the different colours were to come; the third printed the copies in black and white; and the fourth coloured them by hand.

Mrs Elizabeth Stone in her book *The Art of Needlework*, edited by the Countess of Wilton and published in 1840, describes how the German printseller Ludwig Wilhelm Wittich started to use his wife's designs for these patterns and had established a flourishing business by 1810. He was also a painter, engraver and etcher in his own right.

INSTRUCTIONS

These beautiful little Victorian motifs lend themselves to many small embroidery projects. A group of three or four of these designs worked on a fine canvas, 22 stitches to 2.5 cm (1 in) would make a delightful set of pictures. A single motif could be made into a pincushion for a special gift, or set into the lid of a wooden trinket box.

Materials

Single canvas, 16 stitches to 2.5 cm (1 in). You will need 10 x 10 cm (4 x 4 in) of canvas for each project. Their sizes vary slightly but they can all be worked within 10 cm (4 in) square. If you would like to make a matching set the amount of background can be altered to even up the sizes. Allow an extra 7.5 cm (3 in) all around for making up.

For a really fine embroidery that will give the effect of the original, use a smaller-mesh canvas, 18 or 22 stitches to 2.5 cm (1 in).

Use two or three strands of Appleton crewel wool in the needle, depending on your tension. Practise a small area first to see which is sufficient to cover the canvas. If you use three strands allow extra yarn.

You will need one skein of each colour used in the pattern you select and four skeins of 351 for the background. It is important to remember that you should buy all the wool for the background in one go. The dye varies slightly from lot to lot and any change will show up on the background. If you do need to buy a second quantity mix the old batch with the new.

Size 20 or 22 tapestry needles for a 16- and 18-thread canvas; size 22 or 24 for a 22-thread canvas. Use a needle which will take the correct number of threads without damaging them, and which will not distort the canvas when stitching.

Method of working

Fold the canvas in half twice to find the centre. Mark the folds with a hard pencil or tacking stitches. The choice of frame (see page 121) is very much for the individual

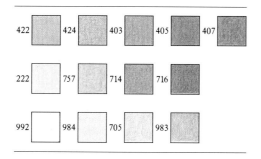

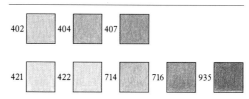

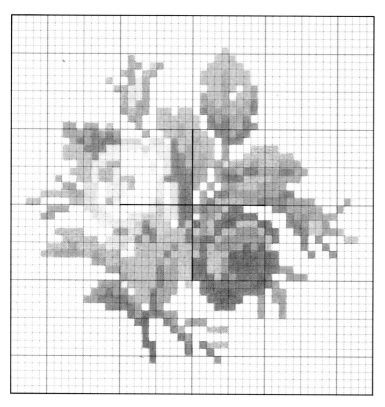

worker. A small square frame would be best if all the motifs are worked together, but if only one is to be embroidered a ring frame will be satisfactory provided the canvas is very tight.

Match your threads to the colour chart key. Find the centre of the chart. Each coloured square on the chart represents one tent stitch or cross stitch. Tent stitch is worked over a single thread of the canvas, but cross stitch could be worked over two threads, i.e. the finished design will be twice the size of a design worked in tent stitch (see page 122 for stitching instructions). Thread a needle with the colour used at the centre of the chart. Knot the end of the thread and take the needle down through the canvas about 5 cm (2 in) from the start of the work. This thread can then be worked over at the back of the canvas as

the embroidery progresses, and the knot cut off. Finish off threads in the same way by bringing each thread up 5 cm (2 in) from the embroidery and these will be worked in.

Complete each design before working the background up to it.

Use a length of wool in the needle not longer than 80 cm (32 in). If the thread is too long, it becomes worn and thin as you work and will not cover the canvas properly.

Further suggestions

---

1   Add highlights to the design by substituting stranded cotton for the palest shade

of wool. Alternatively the whole design could be worked in stranded cotton threads with either a wool or cotton background.

2   These little motifs would be rather nice with a two-colour striped background, but it would have to be very dainty and not overpower the design; for example, four rows of tent stitch in one colour and one row in a slightly darker shade.

3   The little rose motifs would be very nice for a young needleworker to work, and set in a small cushion as a gift for a grandmother or aunt. They are not too difficult for a beginner and more individual and 'grown up' than a kit. Work on larger canvas, 10 stitches to 2.5 cm (1 in), and use four or five strands in the needle.

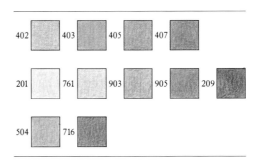

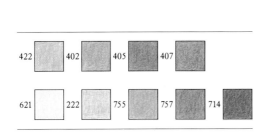

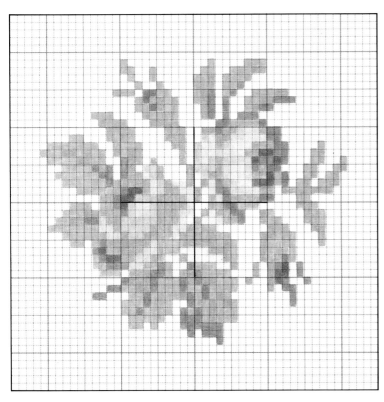

Victorian Sampler

A detail from a sampler worked on a long strip of narrow canvas during the first half of the nineteenth century.

The edges of the sampler are bound with green velvet. At one end there is a piece of black velvet embroidered with yellow silk in floral designs and lined with black satin. Originally a wooden roller covered with black satin was attached to one end and two olive green silk ribbons to the other. The sampler is worked in wool, silk and silver gilt threads and gilt metal beads. The stitches include cross and long-armed cross-stitch, satin, herringbone, back, brick, darning stitch, Hungarian point, laid and couched work. A great variety of floral and geometric motifs has been used with other patterns.

Berlin wool work samplers, such as this one, show a range of the stitches used by more advanced amateurs. These samplers were worked by professionals for amateurs to copy, and often took the form of a small book or a narrow strip which was rolled up and kept in a work box.

Of the more elaborate stitches, lace stitch looked like a border of black silk lace applied to the edge of a table mat, while plush stitch, also called velvet stitch, was achieved by densely working loops which were held to the base fabric with cross-stitch before being cut and trimmed so that the end result looked like padded velvet. Leviathan stitch was used to cover ground quickly as it was a double cross-stitch which was worked over four squares of canvas. It was also known as railway stitch because of the great speed at which it could be worked.

INSTRUCTIONS

The little patterns worked upon this Victorian sampler are very versatile. These simple repeat designs can be worked in cross stitch or tent stitch on chair seats, cushions, waistcoats, slippers, bags, and so on.

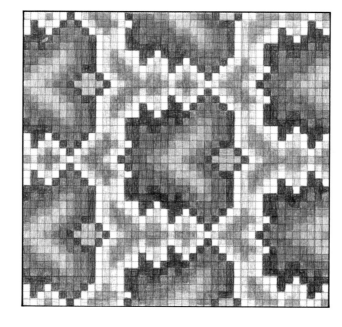

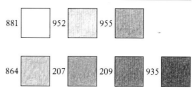

Materials

Single canvas, 16 stitches to 2.5 cm (1 in). The amount of canvas you require will vary according to how you use the design (see page 123 for adapting a chart). Calculate the size of the project you wish to make, and add 7.5 cm (3 in) of canvas all around for making up the finished embroidery.

Use two or three strands of Appleton crewel wool or stranded cotton in the needle for the coloured areas (wool wears best). Practise a small area first to see if this is sufficient to cover the canvas. If you use three strands allow extra yarn.

The quantities of wool required for any of the patterns in this project will depend on how you choose to use the design. The general rule to calculate the amount of wool you need is that one hank will cover an area of 15 x 15 cm (6 x 6 in).

Size 20/22 tapestry needles.

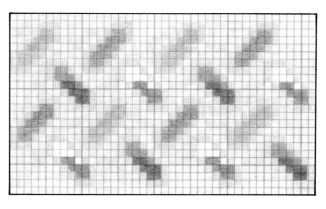

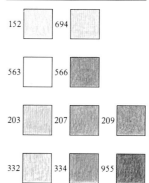

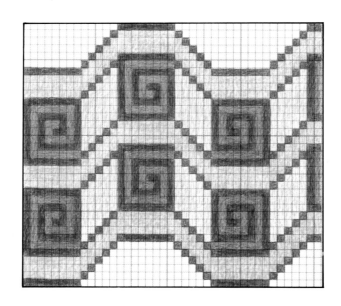

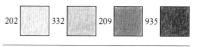

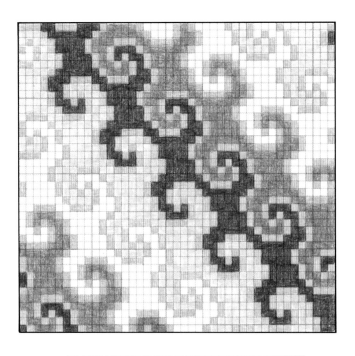

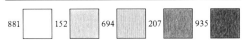

881		152		694		207		935	

Method of working

Fold the canvas in half twice to find the centre. Mark the folds with a hard pencil or tacking stitches. These patterns are best worked in a square peg frame or deep-sided ring frame (see page 121).

Match the coloured threads to the colour chart key. Find the centre of the chart. Each coloured square on the chart represents one tent stitch or cross stitch (see page 122 for stitching instructions).

Thread a needle with the colour used at the centre of the chart. Knot the end of the thread and take the needle down through the canvas about 5 cm (2 in) from the start of the work. This thread can then be worked over at the back of the canvas as the embroidery progresses, and the knot can be cut off. Finish off threads in the same way by bringing each thread up 5 cm (2 in) from the embroidery and these will be worked in.

Use a length of wool in the needle not longer than 80 cm (32 in). If the thread is too long, it becomes worn and thin as you work and will not cover the canvas properly.

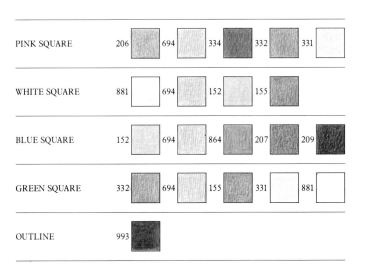

PINK SQUARE	206		694		334		332		331	
WHITE SQUARE	881		694		152		155			
BLUE SQUARE	152		694		864		207		209	
GREEN SQUARE	332		694		155		331		881	
OUTLINE	993									

King Charles Spaniel

A King Charles spaniel, worked in berlin wools on flannel in *circa* 1850.

Household pets were a favourite subject for embroidered pictures, and many paintings of animals were translated into berlin wool work patterns, among them Landseer's *The Macaw, Lovebirds, Terrier and Spaniel Puppies belonging to Her Majesty*. Indeed, Queen Victoria's pets had a great public following and were reproduced in many graphic forms. She was said to be particularly fond of her King Charles spaniel, Dash, the type of dog depicted here. Although this pattern was not based on an original Landseer, it does have the same naturalism and accurate observation that is evident in his work. Comparatively simple pictures of dogs and cats curled up on decorative cushions in this way sold well.

This piece was stitched through both the canvas and the flannel base. Then, once the embroidery had been finished, the loosely woven canvas threads were withdrawn. This much older technique was described in 1770 by Charles Germain de Saint-Aubin, who was embroiderer to Louis XV. He explained how canvas can be placed over a rich silk cloth and the motifs worked, then how the canvas is cut away around the edge of the motif and the threads withdrawn. He also described the techniques of gros and petit point and said that some furniture suppliers sold canvas with the difficult areas of the pattern already completed so that the amateur could fill in the remaining simple areas and have the panels used as upholstery.

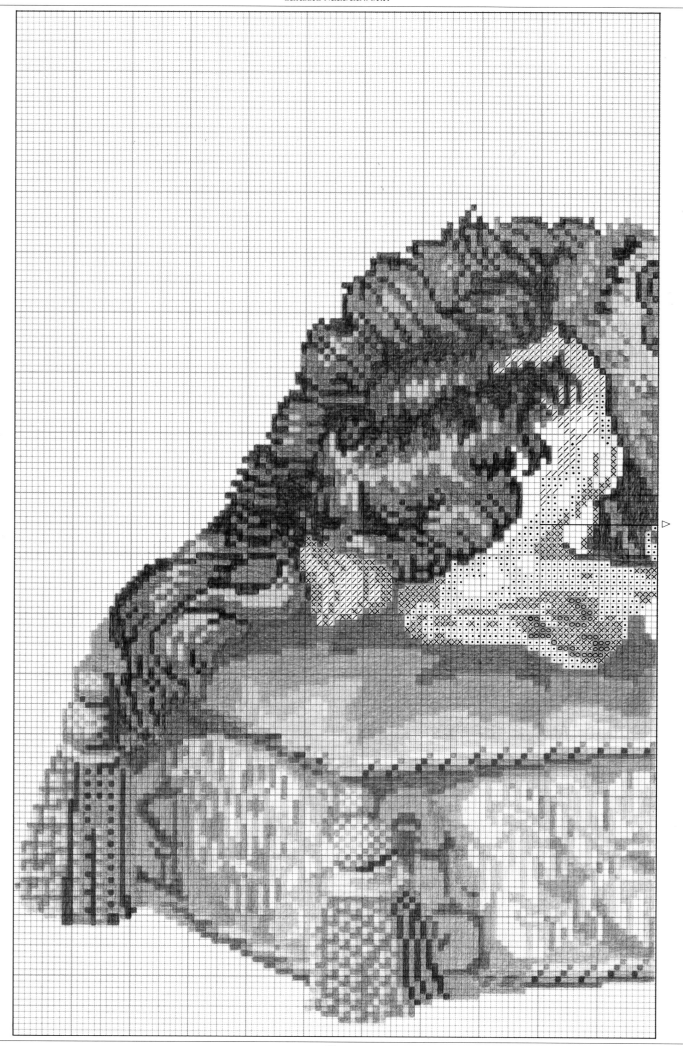

INSTRUCTIONS

This charming little embroidery was originally worked in cross stitch, but can equally well be worked in tent stitch. As the dog is very much a 'one way up' design, it is most suited for use as a picture or perhaps a cushion. (See page 125 for instructions on how to frame a canvas work design.)

If you are working a design such as this with a lot of colours, it is a good idea to thread several needles with different shades as this will save time.

Materials

Single canvas, 16 stitches to 2.5 cm (1 in) for tent stitch, or double canvas, 16 to 2.5 cm (1 in) for cross stitch. You will need 40.5 x 30.5 cm (17 x 12 in) of canvas for tent stitch, which allows for 5 cm (2 in) of background around the design, and extra for cross stitch (see how to adapt a chart page 123). Add an extra 7.5 cm (3 in) all around for making up.

If you like working on fine canvas, 22 stitches to 2.5 cm (1 in) would make a nice picture, worked in tent stitch).

Use two or three strands of Appleton crewel wool in the needle. Practise a small area first to see if this is sufficient to cover the canvas. You may need to use three strands, in which case allow extra yarn.

The quantities of wool given below are approximate and will vary from person to person. It is important to buy the background wool in hanks, rather than skeins, and that each hank is from the same dye lot. The dye varies slightly from lot to lot and any change will show up on the background. If you do need to buy a second quantity then you will need to mix the old batch with the new.

One skein of 127, 223, 226, 291A, 302, 503, 767, 962, 964 and 966; two skeins of 202, 291, 298, 989 and 991B; three skeins of 187, 294, 588 and 766 and three hanks of 881 for the background.

If you wish to extend the background area and use more wool the general rule is that one hank will cover an area of 15 x 15 cm (6 x 6 in).

Size 20/22 tapestry needles.

Method of working

Fold the canvas in half twice to find the centre. Mark the folds with a hard pencil or tacking stitches. A square peg frame should ideally be used for this piece of work, or a deep-sided ring frame (see page 121).

Match your threads to the colour chart key and number if necessary. Find the centre of the chart. Each coloured square on the chart represents one tent stitch or one cross stitch (see page 122 for stitching instructions).

Thread a needle with the colour used at the centre of the chart. Knot the end of the thread and take the needle down through the canvas about 5 cm (2 in) from the start of the work. This thread can then be worked over at the back of the canvas as the embroidery progresses, and the knot then cut off. Finish off threads in the same way by bringing each thread up 5 cm (2 in) from the embroidery and these will be worked in.

Use a length of wool in the needle not longer than 80 cm (32 in). If the thread is too long, it becomes worn and thin as you work and will not cover the canvas properly.

Stitch outwards from the centre of the design. Complete the design before working the background up to it.

Further suggestions

1 Use stranded cotton instead of wool for the lighter shades of the dog's coat. This will give the fur a silky shine, and make the dog stand out against the wool background.

2 Work the background in a stripe or small Florentine stitch (see page 122) to create an interesting contrast.

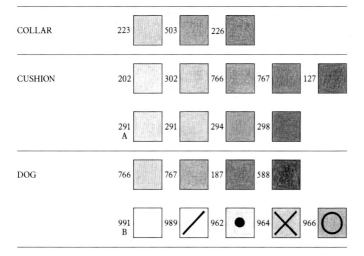

Please note: many subtle shades are used in the chart, therefore the colours for each separate element of the design have been listed individually in the key.

Materials and Techniques

Canvas

Most of the original embroideries illustrated in this book would have been worked on hemp or linen. The canvas we use today is made of different fibres, from man-made materials and plastic to conventional canvas, made of linen or cotton. The very best canvases are made of polished cotton.

Canvas is available in two main weaves — single (mono) and double (Penelope). Single canvas is the most popular and can be purchased in a range of sizes, determined by the number of threads woven to 2.5 cm (1 in). Single canvas has been suggested for most of the designs in this book and is most suitable for tent stitch. It is very clear and easy to see when working a design. Double canvas has pairs of threads woven together each way, and is usually graded by the number of holes to 2.5 cm (1 in). It is ideal for working cross stitch rugs. It also has the great advantage of being able to be split to give four times the number of threads. It is ideal for working fine, detailed designs or for combining coarse and fine work in the same piece of embroidery.

Canvas comes in quite a large range of sizes. A 10-gauge canvas would be 10 holes to 2.5 cm (1 in). Double canvas is available in sizes 7, 8, 9, 10, 14 and 16 stitches to 2.5 cm (1 in). Single canvas is available in sizes 10, 12, 13, 14, 16, 18, 22 and 24 stitches to 2.5 cm (1 in). Fine silk single canvas is also available in sizes 20, 24, 30 and 38 stitches to 2.5 cm (1 in).

It is most advisable to buy a good-quality canvas; it will wear better and be easier to stitch. Knots and slubs make it difficult to get a good tension, and the slubs wear the embroidery wool when working.

White canvas can show through the stitching so brown is preferable.

Always buy enough canvas to allow at least 7.5 cm (3 in) extra all around the design, for framing up, stretching and making up upholstery.

Trim the selvedge as this tends to be tight and will prevent you from getting the canvas taut on the frame.

Threads

Wools

There are many brands of embroidery wool on the market and most embroiderers have their favourite.

Our choice of wool is Appleton crewel wool. This is a two-ply yarn which is quite fine but strong and wears well. The range of colours is wonderful, and, because it is fine, extra shades can be made by mixing different colours in the needle; it also enables you to have exactly the right number of strands in the needle to cover the canvas. Thicker tapestry wool does not always cover as well; one thread may not be enough and two is too thick.

Appleton crewel wools are available in two different quantities — hanks which weigh 25 g (just under 1 oz) and skeins which are $\frac{1}{8}$ of a hank. These are the two quantities used in the book. In addition, some needlework shops will divide the wool into other lengths for you, and sell half hanks and skeins of a $\frac{1}{4}$ and $\frac{1}{6}$ of a hank.

The quantities given for each project are approximate calculations based on the fact that one hank of 25 g (just under 1 oz) covers an area of 15 x 15cm (6 x 6 in). You may want to buy a small amount of each wool initially until you see how much you use. However, it is important to remember that you should always buy the background colour in one batch to avoid dye changes. If you do run low and need more background wool, mix the original wool with the new batch in your needle, to help blend the two together.

Stranded cottons and silks

It is not advisable to use cottons and silks for projects which will have a lot of wear, but they can be added to highlight a piece of work. These threads are also more expensive than wool.

Needlework shops

Appleton crewel wools are sold in most needlework shops in the United Kingdom, and in shops around the world. A selection of suppliers are listed below, but further addresses can be obtained from the Appleton Bros. Ltd, Thames Works, Church Street, Chiswick, London W4 2PE (*Tel 081 994 0711*).

United Kingdom

London
Bridge Embroidery Company
288 Battersea Park Road,
London SW11 3BP

Creativity
45 New Oxford Street,
London WC1A 1BH

Frances Cotton
11 The Market, Greenwich,
SE10 9HZ

W.H.I. Ltd
85 Pimlico Road, SW1 W8PH

Berkshire
Choices
10 Reading Road, Pangbourne,
Reading, Berks RG8 7LY

Cheshire
Voirrey Embroidery
Brimstage Hall, Wirral,
Cheshire L63 6JA

Clwyd
Lalla Thomas
413/415 Abergele Road,
Old Colwyn, Colwyn Bay,
Clwyd LL29 9PR

County Down
Busybodies
Audley Court, 120 High Street,
Holywood, Co. Down BT18 9HW

Cumbria
Russell's Needlework
34 Castle Street, Carlisle,
Cumbria CA3 8TP

Dumfriesshire
Sarah Jane Needlework
110 Drumlanrig Street, Thornhill,
Dumfries DG3 5LU

East Sussex
The Puncheons Craft Studio
73 High Street, Uckfield,
E. Sussex TN22 1AP

Essex
In Stitches
48 Kings Road, Brentwood,
Essex CM14 4DW

Gloucestershire
Ladies Work Society
Delabere House, New Road,
Moreton-in-Marsh,
Gloucestershire GL56 9DD

Hampshire
The Tapestry Centre
42 West Street, Alresford,
Hants SO24 9AU

Hertfordshire
Craft of Stortford
3 the Dells, South Street,
Bishops Stortford,
Herts CM23 3YB

Kincardineshire
Christine Riley
53 Barclay Street, Stonehaven,
Kincardineshire AB3 2AR

Lothian
The Embroidery Shop
51 William Street,
Edinburgh EH3 7LW

Mid Glamorgan
Siop Jen
36/38 Castle Arcade, Cardiff,
S. Glamorgan CF1 2BW

Norfolk
The Handworkers Market
18 Chapel Yard, Albert Street,
Holt, Norfolk NR25 6HG

Oxfordshire
*Royal School of Needlework
Mail Order* Little Barrington,
Burford, Oxon OX18 4TE

Somerset
Arts & Interiors
46/48 Princes Street, Yeovil,
Somerset BA20 1RQ

Surrey
Needle & Thread
80 High Street, Horsell,
Woking, Surrey

Warwickshire
Crafts 'n' Sew On
1427 Pershore Road, Stirtchley,
Birmingham, Warwicks B30 2JL

West Yorkshire
Spinning Jenny
Bradley Keighly,
W. Yorkshire BD20 9DD

Wiltshire
Mace & Nairn
89 Crane Street, Salisbury,
Wiltshire SP1 2PY

USA

California
Needlepoint Inc.
251 Post Street (second floor),
San Francisco, CA 94108

Potpourri Etc
PO Box 78, Redondo Beach,
CA 90277

Delaware
The Jolly Needlewoman
5810 Kennett Pike, Centerville,
DE 19807

Louisiana
Needle Works Ltd.
4041 Tulane Avenue,
New Orleans, LA 70119

Maryland
The Elegant Needle Ltd.
7945 MacArthur Blvd.,
Cabin John, MD 20818

Missouri
Sign of the Arrow
1867 Foundation,
9740 Clayton Road, St. Louis,
MO 63124

New York
American Crewel & Canvas Studio
PO Box 453, 164 Canal Street,
Canastota, NY 13032

Ohio
Louise's Needlework
45 N. High Street, Dublin,
OH 43017

Tennessee
Metamorphosis Inc.
1108 Tyne Blvd., Nashville,
TN 37220

Texas
Chaparral
3701 West Alabama, Suite 370,
Houston, TX 77027

Australia

Altamira
34 Murphy Street, South Yarra,
Melbourne, Victoria 3141

Clifton H Joseph & Son (Australia) Pty. Ltd.
391-393 Little Lonsdale Street,
Melbourne, Victoria 3000

P L Stonewall & Co. Pty. Ltd.
(Flag Division),
52 Erskine Street, Sydney,
New South Wales

Canada

Dick & Jane
2352 West 41st Avenue,
Vancouver, B.C. V6M 2A4

Fancyworks
104-3960 Quera Street,
Victoria, B.C. V8X 4A3

Jet Handicrafts Studio Ltd.
1847 Marine Drive,
West Vancouver, B.C. V7V 1J7

One Stitch At A Time
PO Box 114, Picton,
Ontario K0K 2T0

France

La Passe Recompose
10 Rue des Prebendes,
64100 Bayonne, France

Kell's Corner
82 rue du Cherche Midi,
75008 Paris, France

New Zealand

Nancy's Embroidery Ltd
326 Tinakori Road, PO Box 245,
Thorndon, Wellington

South Africa

Mirza Agencies
PO Box 28741, Sunnyside,
0132, Pretoria

Needlepoint
Box 662 Northlands,
2116 Johannesburg

Photo Zaal
PO Box 1390, 30 Goldman Street,
Florida 1710, Johannesburg

Square peg frames can be ordered from The Royal School of Needlework Mail Order at Little Barrington (see above).

Needlework packs of the embroideries at Traquair House (see page 27) are available by mail order from Traquair House, Innerleithen, Peeblesshire EH44 6PW

Needles

Tapestry needles

Tapestry needles with blunt ends and long eyes are the best needles for canvas embroidery. They are available in a range of sizes from size 18, the largest, to size 26, super-fine.

Use a needle that will take the correct number of threads without damaging them, and that will not distort the canvas when stitching.

Sewing equipment

Scissors

Two pairs of scissors are usually needed — a large general-purpose pair for cutting out the canvas and a small embroidery pair for cutting threads.

Quick-unpick

Used very carefully on the back of the work, this can be helpful if you make a mistake.

Tweezers

These are useful to remove thread ends and fluff from an unpicked area.

Thimbles

These are a 'must'. If you are working on an embroidery frame, wear a thimble on each hand.

Frames

Working on a frame may mean the work will not need stretching when it is finished; it will also allow you to work with both hands, one on top of the work and one underneath, which will speed the work up. Perhaps the most important advantage is that the stitches will have a more even tension than work done in the hand.

There are many different kinds of frame on the market, but the most efficient to use is the square frame with pegs. Although it seems a little cumbersome, it will keep the canvas taut and square.

Alternatively ring frames with deep sides can be used but you will need to move the work round and this may distort the canvas. Work in a ring frame will have to be stretched.

Avoid square travel frames with wing nuts or screws. They are impossible to get tight, and the side arms are so short that the work has to be rolled round the bar many times.

Framing up

To frame up your project on a square frame, you will need two lengths of webbing the width of the work, a ball of string, a large packing needle and some button thread.

1 Fold under a 1.5 cm ($\frac{1}{2}$ in) turning on the top and bottom of the canvas, and mark the centre of this fold with a pin. Mark the centre of the frame webbing with a pin. Put the two pins together and continue to pin the fabric to the webbing all the way along the bar.

2 Oversew from the centre out on both edges. This preparation ensures the fabric is straight on the frame.

3 Place the arms through the bars and tighten the frame by positioning the pegs.

4 When the frame is tight, stitch the webbing with upright tacking down each side of the canvas. The webbing is two-thirds on the canvas and one-third off.

5 Using a large packing needle, brace the sides of the canvas with string through the webbing. Leave a length of string each end; take this string round the frame arms and secure with a slip knot.

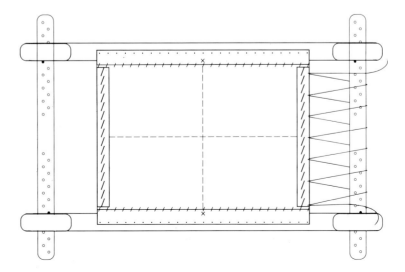

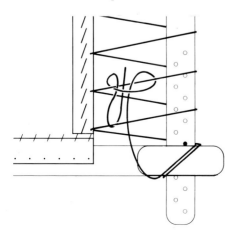

Stitches

The stitches in this book are all traditional canvas embroidery stitches. Many more stitches can be found in other books.

Canvas work is often incorrectly called tapestry work. Tapestries are woven on a loom, not worked with a needle and embroidery stitches.

Every embroiderer works with a different tension, so practise a small area of the design on the side of the canvas. Increase the number of threads if necessary to cover the canvas.

Tent stitch

Tent stitch is one of the two main stitches used in this book, also known as petit point, gros point and half cross stitch. It is the most versatile of all the canvas stitches. The fineness of tent stitch allows you to draw your own design on the canvas in gentle steps and curves, and it is the nearest you will get to the pencil line of the original design.

Tent stitch is worked on the slant across the crossing threads of the canvas, and should have a long stitch on the back of the work —slightly longer on the back than the stitch on the front.

A background in tent stitch is easier to work on the cross of the canvas, as it distorts the canvas less and looks neat. This is called diagonal tent stitch or, in some cases, basket weave tent stitch (the name comes from the appearance of the work on the back). Stitch complete rows from the design to the edge of the work. Wherever possible, take your needle down against your previous work, to help give the embroidery a neat finish.

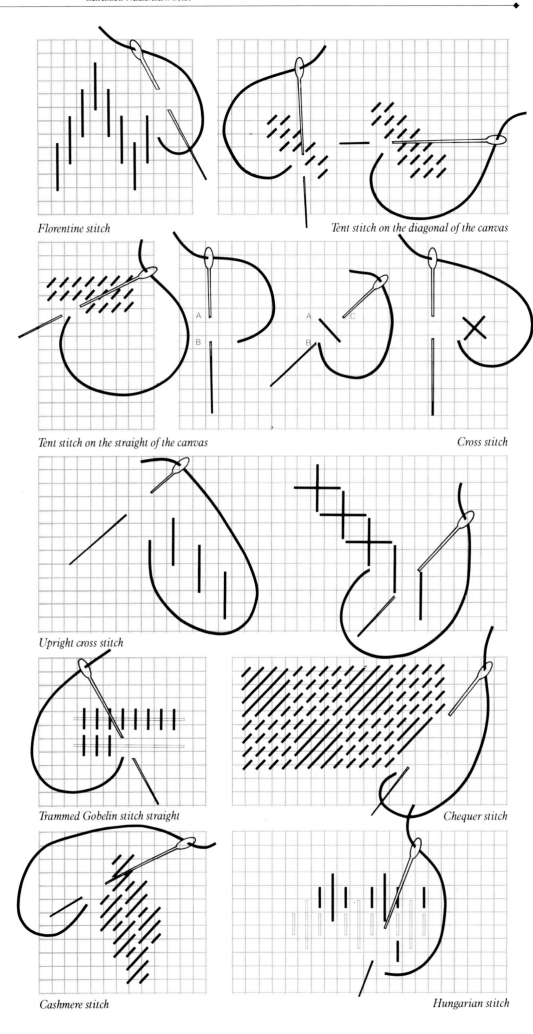

Florentine stitch

Tent stitch on the diagonal of the canvas

Tent stitch on the straight of the canvas

Cross stitch

Upright cross stitch

Trammed Gobelin stitch straight

Chequer stitch

Cashmere stitch

Hungarian stitch

Florentine stitch

This is the other main stitch used in this book, sometimes referred to as bargello. It is a straight stitch worked over several threads of canvas, and 'steps' up or down as the work progresses. The lovely shaded effect is achieved by adding a different colour thread to each row of the work.

Other needlework stitches

These are included mainly to give a variety to the backgrounds. They add texture and make a change for the embroiderer. Be very careful not to overpower a piece of embroidery with a heavy stitch which does not butt up to the tent stitch neatly.

The following stitches are all suitable for using on backgrounds: cross stitch, Hungarian stitch, chequer stitch, cashmere stitch, straight Gobelin stitch and upright cross stitch.

It is a very good idea to try out all the stitches on a spare piece of canvas, then you can choose the one you like best.

Making a template

An upholsterer will supply you with a template of your project (chair seat, stool top, etc.) You can, however, make your own, using a piece of unbleached calico.

1 Fold the calico in half both ways. Mark the centre in both directions, horizontally and vertically.

2 Find the centre of the chair seat or stool top by measuring carefully. Mark the lines with tacking stitches or tailor's chalk.

3 Take into consideration the depth of any extra padding that might be needed when the seat is finally re-upholstered.

4 Lay the calico on the seat, matching the lines to make sure it is quite straight.

5 Smooth the calico out to the edge of the seat. Mark carefully round the outside edge where the existing cover is turned in, using pins or tacking stitches.

6 Remove the template from the seat and tidy up the outline, checking that the shape is symmetrical. Cut out the template.

7 Tack or draw centre lines on the canvas in both directions. Place the template on the canvas. Match the lines on both fabrics, working from the centre outwards.

8 Mark round the edge of the template with a hard pencil or with a line of tacking stitches.

9 Always keep your template for reference. You may need to check whether you have worked enough background to cover the seat.

How to adapt a chart

Each square on the chart represents one stitch, worked over the intersection of two threads of canvas.

Working from a chart instead of a printed canvas means that you can adapt the design if you wish to create a unique piece of embroidery for your own home.

Suggestions for different sizes of canvas are given for each project but if you do want to adapt a design it is very simple to calculate how much you will need for a particular shape. For example, if the chart has 250 squares and you want to make a 45 cm (18 in) cushion, divide 250 by 18 =13.8. The nearest size of canvas is 14 stitches to 2.5 cm (1 in). See page 120 (**Threads**) for advice on how to calculate the amount of yarn you will need.

If a chair seat or cushion is slightly larger than the design, extend the background.

Some projects, especially the Florentine designs, can be embroidered in other colours to match the decoration of a particular room. Follow the subtly graduated shades from light to dark, but using different colours. Paint or crayon your version of the design on graph paper, and work a sample before you start the project.

You may want to use only part of a design, for example, the centre picture of the shepherdess (see page 70) as a framed picture.

If you want to add a border to one of the designs, use one of the patterns in the Victorian Sampler project (see page 110).

Stretching finished embroidery

Even if you have worked the embroidery on a square peg frame, it may be necessary to stretch it back into a true square. To do this, you will need a large piece of wood such as an old drawing board or table top, something you will not mind knocking carpet tacks into. Be sure it does not have a wood stain that will seep into your work when it is damp.

Lay several layers of old towelling on the wood, followed by a piece of old sheeting, both larger than the finished embroidery.

If possible, line up the embroidery with the right-angled corner of the board. Start nailing carpet tacks on the spare canvas from the right-angled corner, working outwards in both directions. Use the edge of the board to make sure the work is straight and tight. The carpet tacks should be not more than 2.5 cm (1 in) apart and just far enough into the wood to hold. Using a set square and ruler, pull and tack the remaining two sides in place, checking and re-checking to see that the work is quite square, even and taut.

Dampen the work all over and leave to dry slowly for two or three days. Extra nails may be needed if they seem too far apart to hold the canvas properly.

When the work is quite dry, remove the tacks. The embroidery should be flat and square, but some pieces are so badly pulled in working that it may be necessary to stretch the work several times before it is quite straight.

Making up a cushion

Many of the designs in this book could be made into cushions. Use a good-quality furnishing fabric or cotton velvet to back the embroidery, choosing a colour that will enhance the finished work. It is important to make the cushion with care; you have spent a lot of hours creating the embroidery, and it would be a pity to spoil everything with poor making-up or fabric.

1 It is not essential to use a zip. A pad sewn neatly into the bottom edge of a cushion would look better than a badly inserted zip. Re-stitch after drycleaning.

2 If you would like a zip, you may find it easier to insert in the middle of the back, before attaching it to the cushion. Cut the backing material in half, and seam together 4 cm ($1\frac{1}{2}$ in) each end of this centre seam. Tack in the zip by hand. Machine or hand stitch in place. By inserting the zip across the back, you will avoid having to juggle with piping, cushion seams and zips all at once.

3 Decide how the edge of the cushion is to be finished off. The two alternatives are piping or a cord.

4 The fabric for the back should be suitable for the piping. Cut the piping fabric on the cross of the material. Cut strips of fabric 5 cm (2 in) wide, as many as are needed to go round the cushion.

5 Join crossway strips and press the seams. Make up the piping with pre-shrunk piping cord. Fold the piping material over the cord and sew this on, keeping close to the cord.

6 Tack the piping round the right side of the embroidery, starting at the centre of the bottom edge. When the ends meet, splice the ends of the cord and join the bias strip.

7 Place the backing fabric (with the zip sewn in) right side down on the right side of the embroidery. Tack through the backing, piping and embroidery. Using a backstitch or piping foot on your machine, stitch all round the cushion. Trim the seam and turn to the right side.

The alternative to piping is to make up the cushion and stitch a cord round the edge. Cord can be obtained from most curtain-making shops.

Upholstery

It would not be wise to give advice on upholstering your finished embroidery. It would be better to have your chair seat or stool top inspected by an expert upholsterer to make sure the webbing and padding are satisfactory. Too much work will have gone into the embroidery to risk cutting or damaging it through inexperience.

Most education authorities run upholstery classes and this would be the best way to get work mounted, with careful help and guidance while learning to carry out your own upholstery.

Mounting embroidery to make a picture

Check the work to see if it needs to be stretched first (see page 124).

1 Cut a piece of heavy card the size of the finished embroidery.

2 Now cut a piece of unbleached calico 7.5 cm (3 in) larger all round than the card.

3 Mitre (cut at an angle) the corners of the calico and bring them and the turnings up onto the card. Glue the edge of the calico onto the card, and leave to dry.

4 Lay the covered side of the board on the wrong side of the embroidery. Trim the extra canvas, leaving about 2.5 cm (1 in) to turn down onto the back of the board. Pin into the edge of the board, positioning the work accurately over the board.

5 Cut away the surplus canvas, leaving enough to mitre the corners neatly.

6 Herringbone stitch the canvas down onto the calico as neatly as possible, just inside the glued edge.

7 When you are satisfied that the work is quite square, back it with a piece of calico and slip stitch it in place.

The embroidery is now ready for framing.

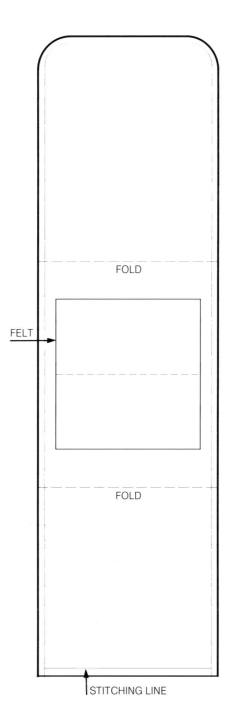

FOLD

FELT

FOLD

STITCHING LINE

Making a needlecase

How to make up a needlecase for the project on page 86.

1 Find a piece of cotton lining material that complements the colours used in the embroidery. With a template the size of the finished embroidery, cut out the lining material — adding $\frac{1}{2}$cm ($\frac{1}{4}$in) turning all round. Cut a piece of 70 g ($2\frac{1}{2}$ oz) polyester wadding the same size as the lining.

2 Now trim down the extra canvas on the embroidery to $\frac{1}{2}$ cm ($\frac{1}{4}$ in). All pieces are the same size.

3 Take a square of felt the colour of the lining material, trim round with pinking shears to a square slightly smaller than the width of the finished needlecase. Stitch by hand or machine across the centre of the felt through the lining and the polyester interlining. This piece of felt will be used for housing the needles.

4 Tack the three layers of material together on the finished outline with right sides outside and polyester in the centre.

5 Cut a $1\frac{1}{2}$ cm ($\frac{1}{2}$ in) crossway strip from the lining cotton, making sure it is long enough to go all round the needlecase. Starting from the centre of the bottom edge, stitch the bias strip onto the right side of the embroidery. This will be stronger if done on a machine. Trim all turnings as low as possible.

6 Turn the bias strip down on to the lining and hem carefully in place. Keep the bias strip as narrow and even as possible.

7 Roll up the finished needlecase and stitch a button or fastening on to the top lip of needlecase.

Bibliography

Christie, Grace
Embroidery & Tapestry Weaving
Bath, 1906

Christie, Grace
Samplers & Stitches
London, 1934

Clabburn, Pamela
Samplers
Aylesbury, 1977

Clabburn, Pamela
Beadwork
Aylesbury, 1980

Colby, Averil
Samplers Yesterday and Today
London, 1964

Digby, G W
'Lady Julia Calverley:
Embroideress Part I' *The Connoisseur'*
CXLV pp 82-87, 1960

Digby, G W
Elizabethan Embroidery
London, 1963

Edwards, Joan
Bead Embroidery
London, 1966

Ewles, Rosemary
One Man's Samplers
The Goodhart Collection
London, 1983

Huish, Marcus B
Samplers and Tapestry Embroideries
London, 1913 & Dover, 1970

King, Donald
Samplers
London, 1960

Levey, Santina
The Hardwick Embroideries
London, 1988

Levey, Santina
Discovering Embroidery of the 19th Century
Tring, 1977

Mayorcas, M J
English Needlework Carpets
Leigh-on-Sea, 1963

Morris, B
Victorian Embroidery
London, 1962

Nevinson, J L
Catalogue of English Domestic Embroidery of 16th and 17th Centuries
London, 1950

Nevinson, J L
'Needlework in the Home in the times of Queen Elizabeth and James I'
Embroidery IV, 1936

Nevinson, J L
'English Domestic Embroidery Patterns of the 16th and 17th Centuries'
The Walpole Society Annual
XXVIII, 1939-40

Nevinson, J L
'An Elizabethan Herbarium:
Embroideries by Bess of Hardwick after Woodcuts of Mattioli'
National Trust Year Book, 1975-76

Nevinson, J L
'Stitched for Bess of Hardwick:
Embroideries at Hardwick Hall,
Derbyshire'
Country Life CLIV, 1973

Nevinson, J L
'Embroidered by Queen and Countess'
Country Life CLIX, 1976

Parry, Linda (Ed)
A Practical Guide to Canvas Work from the Victoria & Albert Collection
London, 1987

Swain, Margaret
The Needlework at Traquair
Edinburgh, 1984

Swain, Margaret
The Needlework of Mary Queen of Scots
London, 1973

Swain Margaret
Figures on Fabric
London, 1980

Synge, Lanto
Antique Needlework
Poole, Dorset, 1982

Synge, Lanto
Book of Needlework and Embroidery
London, 1985

Wade, N Victoria
The Basic Stitches of Embroidery
London, 1981

Wardle, Patrick
Guide to English Embroidery
London, 1970

Zulueta, F de
Embroideries of Mary Stewart & Elizabeth Talbot at Oxburgh Hall, Norfolk
Oxford, 1923

Museums and Collections

where examples of canvas

embroidery can be seen

Museums and Public Collections in the UK

Aston Hall, Birmingham, City of Birmingham

Bowes Museum, Barnard Castle, Co. Durham

Burrell Collection, Glasgow

Fitzwilliam Museum, Cambridge

Holyrood House, Edinburgh Royal Collection

Strangers Hall, Norwich

Temple Newsam House, Leeds City Council

Victoria & Albert Museum, London

Several great houses have some good examples of canvas embroidery:

National Trust Houses

Canons Ashby House, Northamptonshire

Clandon Park, Surrey

Hardwick Hall, Derbyshire

Knole House, Kent

Montacute Manor, Somerset

Oxburgh Hall, Norfolk

Saltram House, Devon

Wallington Hall, Northumberland

National Trust for Scotland

Drum Castle, Aberdeenshire

Haddo House, Aberdeenshire

Private Collections

Drumlanrig Castle, Dumfriesshire

Mellerstain House, Berwickshire

Scone Palace, Perthshire

Traquair House, Peeblesshire

Collections in other countries:

USA

The Art Institute of Chicago

Colonial Williamsburg Foundation Virginia

Cooper-Hewitt Museum, New York

The Henry Francis du Pont Winterthur Museum, Delaware

Isabella Stewart Gardner Museum, Boston

Metropolitan Museum of Fine Art, New York

Museum of Fine Arts, Boston

Europe

Het Loo Palace, Netherlands

Musée des Arts Décoratifs, Paris, France

Rijksmuseum, Amsterdam, Netherlands

Index